Swimming for Fitness

Swimming for Fitness

◆

A Guide to Developing a Self-Directed Swimming Program

David A. Grootenhuis

Writers Club Press
San Jose New York Lincoln Shanghai

Swimming for Fitness
A Guide to Developing a Self-Directed Swimming Program

Writers Club Press
an imprint of iUniverse, Inc.

For information address:
iUniverse, Inc.
5220 S. 16th St., Suite 200
Lincoln, NE 68512
www.iuniverse.com

ISBN: 0-595-25300-8 (pbk)
ISBN: 0-595-65081-3 (cloth)

Printed in the United States of America

Contents

Preface

I had been involved with competitive swimming for 16 years when I finished college. In those days college graduation signaled the end of a swimming career. At the age of 21 I felt that I still had a few good races left. I continued training and found competitive venues for swimmers my age. There wasn't a local adult team available, so I began training on my own, during lap swimming sessions at local pools.

I spent considerable time training during lap swims for the next 12 years. I balanced swimming with a professional career and augmenting my training routine by swimming with local high school and age group teams when schedules permitted.

Over the years I got to know a number of the people that came to the pool every day to swim. These were people that swam for the shear exercise value. They were not training for competition, reward or notoriety. They swam for the feeling of a good workout and the health benefits of swimming. I was amazed at their motivation.

They dutifully came to the pool, donned their goggles and set out on a quest for fitness. They had dedication and a sense of purpose that many coaches would admire.

I was surprised to discover that very few of them had a swimming background. Most had taken up swimming purely for exercise. Few had any experience in structuring a swimming program or organizing a workout. They came to the pool and swam their allotted amount of time or specified distance, stopping only to catch their breath of adjust their goggles.

I couldn't imagine swimming the same long session every day. This made me even more impressed with their motivation. At the same time, I thought of how much more they could get out of their workouts if they added some variety to their routines. Their workouts could be so much more beneficial and enjoyable.

After retiring from competition I became a fitness swimmer. I, too, went to the pool regularly for the pure health benefit. I found that some of the techniques I had used when training alone for competition could be used in fitness swimming as well.

So, I wrote a book about it. This text is the culmination of years spent seeking speed, endurance and, eventually, health.

I hope you enjoy it and find it helpful.

Introduction— Swimming in a Fitness Program

Swimming is one of nature's most beneficial forms of exercise. It employs virtually every muscle in the body and improves the body's strength and endurance without overly stressing the joints. Every year more and more people are discovering the benefits of swimming to their health and vitality.

Swimming programs can be designed with a combination of strength and endurance that can be applied to any fitness program. It can assist in weight loss, muscle development and general fitness. It is an effective program that can help people lose weight, get and stay fit and feel great.

The human body has few natural aspects that make it efficient in the water. One need only compare the human silhouette to that of a dolphin for proof. The human lack of efficiency in the water is one of the things that make swimming such good exercise. It takes more effort to move through water than to move through air.

The explosion in the popularity of swimming as form of exercise has attracted people to pools that are inexperienced in developing swimming programs. Few facilities have organized swimming instruction for adults. Unlike weight training or aerobic exercise classes, the pool rarely has a fitness advisor or instructor.

Many of the people that have taken to the pool do so alone. They establish their fitness routine and rely upon their own expertise to create a fitness program. Even experienced swimmers may find themselves without the benefit of an organized "team" environment for the first time.

There are advantages to developing a program tailored to an individual. The workouts can be custom-made to reach specific fitness goals. An individual is free to try new approaches and test results without interfering with anyone else's routine. The schedule is flexible since it only involves one person's calendar. While a group environment may be preferable to some, busy adults often find it difficult to coordinate workout times with a group. A fitness program designed and executed by one person is often the best or only solution.

Chapter One—Personal Fitness Programs

F itness is more than working out. Physical health involves more than just eating the right foods and exercising. Physical fitness is the result of a healthy *lifestyle*. Physical health results from a combination of lifestyle factors. The journey to physical fitness can sometimes involve radical changes in habits.

There are four factors in structuring a fitness program:

- Goals

- Activity

- Nutrition

- Rest

Dieting isn't enough. A fitness program must include all of these factors to be effective.

SETTING GOALS

As with most initiatives, the first step is to establish what is to be accomplished. Understanding your fitness goals will help to keep your program focused and will enable you to measure your progress.

Is your goal to lose weight? Is it to change the way you look? Is it to improve your general level of fitness? Build confidence? Is it to become a better swimmer? It may be all of these. All are examples of very worthy fitness goals and there are many others. It is critical to have an understanding of what your fitness goals are and to recognize the effort necessary to achieve them.

One of the keys to establishing goals is to determine your current fitness level and your ability to commit time to a fitness program. Understand what has motivated you to take on a fitness program. Your goals should be challenging, yet realistic and attainable. An advantage of structuring a program for yourself is that you can easily transition to new goals when you achieve the old ones.

Goals can be a motivational tool to provide inspiration as you work through your program. Goals that are too aggressive can become discouraging. Goals that are too easy to attain may cause a loss of interest in further progress. Goal setting is a good lesson in self-evaluation. Objectively assess your current situation and set goals accordingly.

Understand what you want from your fitness program before setting goals. Very aggressive goals may require greater changes in lifestyle. Achieving the perfect physique requires considerably more commitment than losing a few pounds. Be honest with yourself about the amount of effort that will be required.

Understand the constraints that may be placed on a fitness program. There is a time commitment involved that must be accounted for. The commitment does not have to be burdensome, but it must be recognized. You should be comfortable with the time you wish to commit to the program and realistic about your ability to commit the time.

There is also a financial commitment. Swimming pools usually change some type of fee for use, generally a membership of some kind. You will also need to provide some basic equipment.

The financial and time commitments to a fitness program are investments in improved health and lifestyle. The cost is easily justified by the gains.

The bottom line in setting goals: Be honest with yourself and realistic in your expectations.

ACTIVITY

Activity includes all of the daily motions that make up life. The type of activity involved in your lifestyle has a profound impact on your level of overall health. Activity performs two basic functions: it works the muscles and joints and it uses the energy produced by the food we eat.

Imagine that an automobile were able to expand it's fuel tank to accommodate any amount of fuel. If the car were not driven enough to use all of the fuel that was put into the tank, the car would develop a surplus of fuel. This surplus would be stored in the ever-expanding fuel tank. Eventually, the weight of the fuel may be more than the engine can move.

Another aspect of activity for automobiles is efficiency. A car that is driven infrequently becomes inefficient and sluggish.

The human body behaves in a similar fashion. If the level of activity does not burn the amount of fuel taken in, the body stores the fuel as fatty deposits. Activity also improves the efficiency of the body. With fitness, the muscles become stronger, joints become more flexible and the body turns food into energy more efficiently.

A person's normal level of daily activity may not use all of the fuel provided to the body by food. Additional activities can be added to use the excess and improve efficiency. This additional activity is known as exercise. It has been described as "activity for the sake of activity".

Swimming

Swimming burns a great deal of fuel in a very short time. The human body has few physical characteristics that help it move easily through the water. This lack of efficiency is one of the things that make swimming an excellent form of exercise.

Swimming employs virtually every muscle in the body and improves the body's strength and endurance without overly stressing the joints. It can be the focal point of any fitness program.

Cross Training

Cross training incorporates different types of exercise into a fitness program. Swimming is an excellent training method for other sports. The benefits of strength and conditioning that are derived from swimming can easily be applied to almost any other activity. While swimming is among the most beneficial forms of exercise, it should be noted that any fitness program can include a variety of activities. Cross training allows the body to work the muscle groups in a variety of situations and develop a total body routine.

DIET

The basis of any fitness program is a good diet. The diet is the fuel that the body uses to operate. As with the automobile, the type of fuel used has an impact on performance. A car will run on a number of fuels, but runs best on quality gasoline. The human body will function on about any diet, but functions best on a diet that features a variety of foods and avoids "junk".

This is especially true for swimmers. Swimming burns energy very quickly and the type of fuel provided to the body influences performance in the pool as well as general health. Swimming does not require any special dietary allowances. A varied diet of nutritious foods will suffice. Food with limited nutritional value should be avoided. The body must receive the proper nutrition to support the demands of a training program.

There are a number of popular diet plans designed to assist in weight loss and fitness. This book does not endorse or discourage any of them. This book does endorse adherence to a fundamental dietary plan. It is important to be aware of what is being eaten and the impacts on fitness. The foods chosen for meals and snacks are a key factor in fitness and health.

Fluids are a key part of the diet. Maintaining a proper intake of fluids will help the body eliminate the waste products associated with exercise. Proper fluids help muscles deal with the increased stress of a training program and reduce the stiffness associated with exercise (Note: some muscle stiffness is a good sign. It means that the muscles are working beyond their previous limits. It may hurt, but it's a *good* hurt)

SLEEP

Exercise causes fatigue. Fatigue is normal in any fitness program. Swimming can be especially tiring since it uses the entire body and requires movement through a substance that has a greater density than the air. The proper amount of sleep will help maintain good health and a general feeling of well being. Eight hours per night is a good goal.

THE USUAL WARNINGS

Swimming is a strenuous exercise. Consult with a physician before beginning a new program, especially if you have not recently been involved in a structured fitness program.

Make an objective evaluation of your swimming ability. While swimming is an excellent form of exercise for all skill levels, there are some aspects of safety that must be addressed. Swimming skills will improve dramatically with continued practice, but swimmers must be safe in the water to begin.

Swimming, like many forms of exercise, impacts your metabolism and immune system. As you begin your program, you may find that you are more susceptible to conditions such as a minor cold. This is not unusual. As your body adjusts to the new level of physical activity, your immune system will adjust and the cold will subside.

It is important to note that there is a period of time at the beginning of a fitness program when you may not lose weight or may even gain weight due to increased muscle mass. This is a good thing. It will inevitably cause the body to burn more calories and weight loss will be more dramatic.

GENERAL COMMENTS

Swimming can provide a life-long level of fitness that will enhance your level of energy and lifestyle for many years. There are many examples of individuals that have remained active swimmers well into their nineties. Swimming for fitness or in competition is open to anyone willing to try it. The only minimum requirement is to be safe in the water.

The success of any fitness program is dependent upon these factors:

- The program must have a routine. The worst program is strenuous and irregular. The best program is challenging and routine. The program must involve exercise on a regular basis with a level of difficulty that keeps it challenging.

- The program must be realistic. Being too aggressive too early can become discouraging. Make an objective evaluation of your abilities before setting goals and develop a program to reach those goals.

- The program must be supported by a proper diet and sufficient rest.

Chapter Two—Choosing A Facility

The first step in developing a swimming program is finding a place to swim. The facility chosen has a profound effect on the success of the program. If you are not comfortable with the facility, you may not look forward to going there. The equipment or schedule available at the facility can hinder or enhance your program.

There are a number of factors involved in selecting a facility. To make a choice that you are happy with involves evaluating the options and establishing the criteria in terms of what is important in your situation. Before making your final selection, you must decide which of the criteria you are willing to compromise on and which one you are not. For some, the decision will be driven by a convenient location. These people may be willing to accept a lesser facility that is convenient for them. Others may demand a top quality facility regardless of the location. Since the program is custom designed, the selection is entirely up to the swimmer's criteria.

Location

The location of a facility has a profound impact on your level of satisfaction and willingness to use the facility. Selecting a facility that is close to your home will allow you to work out evenings and weekends, but may limit your ability to exercise during your business hours. A facility convenient to work may support workouts during the day, but may limit evening and weekend sessions.

In evaluating locations, it is also important to consider how difficult it is to get there. A facility that is further away may be more convenient due to traffic or other factors.

Hours

Many of the more desirable pools are used by a number of different groups. Swimming teams, water polo, synchronized swimming, diving, fitness classes or swimming lessons may share the pool. Before choosing a facility, find out when the pool is available for lap swimming.

Cross Training

Many health clubs offer pools as one of many forms of exercise. If you are interested in cross training, find a facility that provides the equipment and expertise to accommodate a variety of forms of exercise. These may include weight training, running, fitness machines and/or organized classes such as aerobics.

Facilities for Children

Many fitness facilities provide a managed area for children. (There is usually a nominal cost involved) This is a great benefit for those who wish to swim and have children that are too young to accompany them.

Swimming Instruction

Most facilities with pools offer some type of swimming instruction, usually for children. Swimming instruction for adults is usually in the form of private lessons. If you feel that some instruction might be appropriate, find out if the facility offers any type of swimming instruction for adults.

POOLS

Exceptional swimming facilities can enhance and encourage the swimming experience. Inadequate facilities can be very frustrating and limit the willingness to continue your program. The impacts of the physical characteristics of a pool are more subtle than dramatic. A well-designed pool seems less crowded, even when it is near capacity. Well-designed pools allow swimmers to concentrate on their workouts, rather then the challenges of their surroundings.

Most pools designed for training are rectangular and 25 yards or 25 meters long. The pool is divided into *lanes* by floating *lane markers* (Also known as *lane lines*). Lane markers are necessary in any pool used for lap swimming. Do not consider any pool that does not use lane markers during lap swimming periods.

Most pools have lines painted on the bottom and ends of pool to identify the lanes. Pools designed for lap swimming have between 6 and 10 lanes, though some may have as few as 4 lanes. The lanes must be wide enough to accommodate two swimmers side-by-side. Lanes should not be less than 7 feet (about 2 meters) wide, 8 feet wide is better.

Pools that are 25 yards or 25 meters long support the standard distances used in competitive swimming. Pools built before the 1950's may be only 20 yards long, since competitive swimming used different distances at that time. "Olympic" pools, which are designed to accommodate international completion, are 50 meters long.

Pool Design

Competitive swimmers refer to certain pools as being "fast". Fast pools have design characteristics that make swimming in them less stressful on the body and therefore, "faster".

The characteristics that make pools fast also make them preferable as a training facility. The key factor is "still" water.

Still water is not in motion when you swim through it. The chief enemy of still water is turbulence. Turbulence is created when anything disturbs the water. They appear on the surface in the form of waves, but also move beneath the surface. They are inevitable when swimming. Turbulence radiate through water in all directions.

Vibrations created by the swimmer bounce off the bottom of the pool and create more turbulence on their way back to the surface. Waves move horizontally through the water and bounce off the sides and ends of the pool to create more waves in the center. Through this process a single swimmer can create a storm of waves in a poorly designed pool.

A well-designed pool has provisions to reduce or eliminate turbulence created by swimmers. One way that pools combat waves is with depth. Turbulence lose strength as they move away from the source of the disturbance. As the vibration moves toward the bottom of the pool it loses intensity. The deeper the water, the weaker the disturbance when it strikes the bottom. The ideal depth of a pool is around eight feet. At a minimum the water should be four feet deep.

The design of the lane markers and gutters impact the pool's ability to deal with waves. Lane markers should absorb the impact of a wave and prevent it from bouncing back onto the lane or crossing into the next lane. Most pools have some type of gutter at the water's edge. Gutters allow overflow water to run out of the pool. The gutters of the pool should be designed to absorb waves and prevent them from bouncing back into the pool. Gutters should be continuous around the pool edge. There should be no point in the pool where a wave may strike a vertical surface. A vertical surface will reflect the wave back into the pool.

Observe the pool as swimmers move through the water. Look for these signs:

- Do the waves created by swimmers pass from one lane to another?

- Do the waves bounce off the walls to create more waves?

- Does the surface of the water in unused lanes appear smooth?

Another good test is to observe the pool when it is empty. Disturb the surface of the water at one end of a center lane and watch the ripples as they spread from that point. The degree to which the waves disappear into the lane markers and gutters indicates the ability of the pool to defuse turbulence.

The Pool Area

Water Clarity

The water in the pool should be clear, as nearly transparent as possible. Swimming in cloudy water is quite difficult. Swimmers must be able to see clearly through the water to avoid collisions with other swimmers and see the end of the pool. A good test is to stand at one end of the pool and look down the lane at the opposite end. If the bottom of the pool at the opposite end can be seen distinctly, the water has the necessary clarity.

Water Temperature

The water in a training pool should feel slightly cool upon entry. The ideal temperature is between 78 and 80 degrees. This is slightly cooler than the temperature in recreation pools. The cooler water is more comfortable when swimming for exercise. Swimmers can overheat in water that is too warm. Water that is too cold will be uncomfortable at any level of activity.

Air Temperature

The air in the pool area of an indoor pool should feel slightly warmer than the rest of the building. This will prevent wet swimmers from feeling chilled when they are not in the water.

Ventilation

An indoor pool should have fresh air flowing into the pool area and stale air flowing out. There can be a scent of chlorine in the air, but it should not be heavy or overpowering. Problems with ventilation are more apparent in facilities build before the mid-1970's.

While outdoor pools can have few problems with fresh air, there can be a problem with too much ventilation. The design of the pool should provide protection from strong winds.

Lighting

Indoor pools should have lighting sufficient to enable the swimmers to see clearly under the water. Lights should be arranged to that they do not shine directly into the swimmers' eyes and do not produce glare on the surface of the water. Swimmers often swim on their backs, looking up at the ceiling. Bright lights should not be placed directly over the swimming lanes. Underwater lighting should not be placed where it will shine directly into the face of a swimmer. Underwater lighting is usually located on the sides of the pool, rather then the ends. If underwater lights are placed at the end of the pool, they should be under the lane marker (between lanes) rather then in the center of the lane. In all cases, indirect lighting is preferable.

Outdoor pools will require lighting if they are available after sunset. The rules above apply to outdoor lighting as well.

Deck Space

The area around the pool is known as the *deck*. The deck should have sufficient space for people to safely walk around the pool. The pool deck is usually wet, so there should be an area for swimmers to put their towels and other equipment where it will remain dry. Benches, bleachers or hooks will suffice.

Inlets

Pool water is kept clean and clear through a continuous filtration system. Water is removed from the pool through the drains and gutters, passed through a filter system and returned to the pool through *inlets*. Inlets are places where water is put into the pool. For the best circulation of the water, inlets should be disbursed throughout the pool. Most pools have inlets in the bottom and/or the walls. Inlets can be designed to disburse the incoming water to minimize turbulence. The inlets should never aim water directly at a swimmer. Wall inlets should be placed under the lane markers. The force of the water entering the pool should not be noticeable by anyone in the water.

Walls

The walls of the pool are used as a starting place and as a place to push against while turning around. The texture of the walls should not be slippery and the walls should have markings that make them easy to see while swimming.

Walls in pools that are more than 5 feet deep should have some type of foothold so swimmers can support themselves while resting.

Pool Chemicals

Chemicals are used in pools to kill the germs that may develop in a damp environment. The most common chemical used for this purpose is chlorine. Chlorine is very effective at keeping pools clear of any unwanted substances. Some pools use Bromine, which is also very effective. New developments include electronic processes that do not require additional chemicals.

It is important to be aware of the chemicals used in the pool system. Some chemicals have side effects on swimmers such as bleached hair and dry skin. Swimmers may also have allergic reactions to some chemicals. Be aware of the chemicals used in any pool prior to purchasing a membership.

Clocks

There are two types of clocks that should be available at the pool. The first is a conventional clock that displays the time of day. This is a convenience to keep everyone on schedule.

The second type of clock in called a *pace clock*. A pace clock is used to regulate the swimming session (known as a *workout*). Pace clocks are available with either analog or digital displays. These clocks should be placed on the side of the pool near each end and be located so that they can be easily seen by swimmers in the water. This allows swimmers to see the clock from all of the lanes. Ideally, there should be four pace clocks, one in each corner of the pool.

All of the pace clocks around the pool should be synchronized. This allows swimmers to monitor their pace without having to rely on a single clock.

Equipment

A facility that has an interest in swimming will usually provide kick boards. Some also supply pull buoys. If the facility does not provide equipment or if the equipment provided is not adequate, swimmers can usually provide their own. Equipment that is provided by the facility should be easily accessible to participants.

A facility that does not provide basic equipment may not have a strong commitment to fitness swimming.

Organization

Crowded pools can be very frustrating places. Well-organized facilities designate lanes based on swimming ability. Lanes in the pool are often designated "Slow", "Medium" and "Fast". Visit the pool at the time of day you plan to swim to see how crowded it is and how the facility deals with the crowd.

Motivation

Many facilities provide motivation to fitness swimmers through organized activities. Some organize fitness swimming groups to record distances for prizes or recognition.

Availability

Prior to selecting a facility, make sure the pool is available at the time of day you plan to swim. Many pools have multiple uses including swimming lessons, fitness classes, synchronized swimming, water polo and swimming team workouts. There are many other potential uses. Find out when the pool is available for fitness swimming (Usually referred to a "lap swimming") and make sure that the times fit your schedule.

Safety

Pool safety is essential. Local regulations usually provide the minimum safety standards for pools that are available for public use. Here are some common safety elements:

- Are lifeguards on duty during lap swim periods?
- Is safety equipment visible in the pool area?
- Are the pool rules posted in the pool area?
- Are the pool rules enforced?
  > Observe the pool area to see if the pool staff is enforcing the posted rules
- Are lanes designated for lap swimming kept clear of recreational swimmers?

Many pools are used for multiple purposes simultaneously. For example, there may be recreational swimming and lap swimming in different sections of the pool. A crowded recreational pool creates a great deal of turbulence. This arrangement can be successful if the pool design can defuse the turbulence, the recreational section of the pool is not overly crowded and the lap swimming lanes are kept clear of recreational swimmers.

General Appearance

Some other points to consider:

- Is pool clean?
- Is the deck area orderly and organized?
- Are the lifeguards watching the activity in the pool?
- Does an indoor pool have windows?

LOCKER ROOMS

The locker room facilities also impact the selection of a facility. Locker rooms should be large enough to comfortably accommodate the number of people that will be using it at the same time. There should also be a sufficient number of showers and restrooms.

Criteria for evaluating locker rooms includes:

- Does the locker room have adequate lighting?
- Does the facility provide locks? (This is a matter of preference. You should know if you need to bring a lock)
- Is the locker room clean?
- Is the floor wet?
- Are there sinks and mirrors?
- Is there diaper changing facilities?
- Are there any problems with water temperature in the showers?

- Do youth and adults have separate facilities?

- Does the locker room have direct access to the pool area? (The pool area is usually warmer than the rest of the building. Direct access prevents wet swimmers from having to walk through other parts of the building that may seem cold)

OTHER FACILITIES

The types of training that can be accommodated at the facility may impact your fitness program. Some facilities may offer only swimming while others are full-service fitness centers. Investigate the training opportunities that are offered by the facility.

OTHER FACTORS

General issues include adequate and convenient parking and the cost of using the facility. It is also important to identify the focus of the establishment. Some facilities are primarily designed for specific types of training and offer others as an accommodation. Some fitness centers attempt to provide equal accommodations for many types of exercise. Try to identify what the primary focus of each facility is before making a final selection.

Ask questions if you have specific concerns about a facility. Perhaps the pool is normally very clear, but is cloudy today because of a mechanical problem. This type of information will only be available if you ask for it.

It is important to note that a membership should be purchased rather than using a pay-per-visit arrangement. In a pay-per-visit environment, there is a tendency to "justify" visits by only working out when a large block of time is available. This can defeat a fitness program. Programs must be challenging and regular, with emphasis on *regular*. A short workout is infinitely better than no workout at all. Purchasing a membership will allow more frequent, if shorter, visits to the facility.

This chapter outlines many of the criteria that can be used to evaluate fitness facilities. Each person developing a fitness program must select their facility based on what is important to them. Not all of the criteria presented here will apply and there may be additional criteria specific to the individual making the choice. Weigh these factors and choose the facility that best fits the situation.

OPEN WATER SWIMMING

Swimming in areas other than pools is referred to as "Open Water Swimming". This includes swimming in lakes, rivers, ponds or the ocean. Swimming in open water can be very beneficial and can also present unique challenges.

Open water swimming differs from swimming in a pool in that there are few boundaries in the open water. There are no walls or lane lines. In open water a swimmer can cover a great distance without having to turn around.

Open water swimming can build a very strong stroke rhythm, as there are few interruptions to the swim. There are no fixed stopping points and there are no walls to force the swimmer to turn around. Uninterrupted swimming allows the swimmer to concentrate on their stroke and breathing.

Open water swimming also helps balance the stroke. Unbalanced strokes occur when one arm is stronger or more efficient than the other. When swimming in a pool a swimmer compensates by altering their body position or their stroke to stay in their lane. In open water an unbalanced stroke will cause a swimmer to swim in a circle.

Many swimmers find that their stroke becomes more efficient when swimming in open water. There is a natural tendency to lengthen the stroke and thus get more propulsion from each pull (Details in Chapter 5 on stroke mechanics).

Equipment such as pull buoys and kick boards can be used in open water. However, it is important to note that these are not approved life saving devices and cannot be depended upon in the event of an emergency.

There are also some challenges to open water swimming. Measurement of distance is difficult. Since there are few guides in open water (there are no lines on the bottom of a lake), swimming in a straight line can also be difficult. This also limits the options for varying workouts.

Swimming in open water also brings in elements that are not factors in pool swimming. Currents in the water can have a profound impact on a swimmer. Wind and waves will affect stroke mechanics and breathing. Even very small waves will force a swimmer to alter their stroke. Boat traffic is a hazard as swimmers can be difficult for boaters to see. Swimming in deep water or a great distance from shore can make it difficult to reach safety in the event of an emergency.

When swimming in open water, be sure to swim in an area that is not frequented by boats. If you hear or see a boat, make sure that the boaters see you. Wearing a brightly colored cap makes swimmers more noticeable. Avoid swimming in areas with a strong current or heavy waves.

Chapter Three—Equipment

The equipment used in swimming has a profound effect on the success of the program. Frustrations with poorly designed or ill-fitting equipment can undermine a well-planned fitness routine.

SWIMWEAR

In selecting swimwear, it is important to note that most swimwear creates resistance as it moves through the water. This resistance is known as "drag". Drag is created two ways. The fabric from which the swimming suit was made could absorb water and become heavy when wet. This adds weight to the swimmer, thus forcing the swimmer to move more weight through the water. The shape of the swimwear is also a factor. If the suit is bulky or billowing in the water, it will affect the body's streamlining and slow a swimmer's progress through the water. It may also catch water as a parachute catches air. These combine to alter the swimmers body position in the water and can severely affect swimming performance.

Some swimming suits have been designed to minimize the effects of drag on the swimmer. Fitness swimmers should wear the same type of suits that are used by competitive swimmers. For men, this is a lightweight suit that resembles briefs. For women, this is a simple, one-piece swimming suit. Competitive suits are made of lightweight fabrics such as lycra or nylon.

GOGGLES

Goggles protect the eyes from the effects of the water as well as improving underwater vision. They should be as small as possible and streamlined to minimize the amount of drag they create. There are a number of types of goggles that can be purchased at most sporting goods stores or swim shops. Note that the more expensive goggles are not necessarily a better product than less expensive models.

Tinted goggles can help protect the eyes from bright sunlight. These goggles have colored lenses similar to sunglasses. Prescription goggles are also available for swimmers who wear glasses.

Goggles should fit snuggly on the eyes, but not tightly. They protect the eye by forming a watertight seal with the skin around the eye. This is accomplished by creating a "suction". To test the fit, place one goggle over one eye and press it lightly into place. If the goggle remains in place momentarily, there is a good seal. Repeat the process with the other eye.

There may be a slight distortion of depth perception when first swimming with a new pair of goggles. This is caused by a refraction of light below the surface of the water. This is not unusual and will subside as the eyes adjust. The adjustment period is usually not more than a few minutes.

Always follow the manufacturer's instructions for the proper way to put on, remove and care for goggles.

A common problem with goggles is their tendency to fog. Fogging is condensation inside the goggle that can make seeing difficult. There are several methods to prevent fogging on the inside of the goggles. A common method is to keep a few drops of water in the goggle to rinse off the fog. This works, but the water inside the goggles may irritate the eyes. There are a number of solutions available commercially that can prevent fogging. Some goggles also have "anti-fog" coatings.

A very effective and inexpensive way to prevent fog is saliva. Place a small amount of your saliva in each goggle and use pool water to rinse it into the gutter. (That's right, spit in the goggle and rinse with pool water into the gutter, it works)

KICK BOARDS

Kick boards are used to support the front of the body in the water while kicking. The body position while kicking should be the same as the body position while swimming. The kick board provides the buoyancy necessary to keep the front of the body in proper alignment.

Kick boards are made of styrofoam, foam rubber or plastic. They are available in a variety of styles, shapes and colors. The size of the kick board is a major factor in its effectiveness. If a kick board is too large, it is difficult to control and may create drag that slows the swimmer in the water. If the board is too small it may not provide the buoyancy necessary to support the body. The most useful kick boards are flat, about 18" long, 12" wide, 1"–2" thick and slightly rounded at the front. Note that a powerful kick can support the upper body with little help from a kick board. Swimmers with strong kicks may opt for smaller kick boards.

When using a kick board for freestyle, butterfly or breaststroke, the arms should be extended over the board with the hands grasping the board at the front. The arms should be in front of the swimmer. The back should be arched with the hips just below the surface of the water. The head should be held slightly more upright than when swimming. Eyes focused ahead and the water breaking over the nose just below the eyes. The swimmer should lift the head to breathe.

The kick board should not be used when kicking baskstroke. The arms should be placed over the head with hands together and elbows straight. The back should be slightly arched to bring the hips just below the surface of the water.

Most pools that emphasize fitness swimming supply kick boards. If not, they are generally available from swim shops or sporting goods stores.

PULL BUOYS

Pull buoys are floatation devices that support the legs during pull sets. Pull sets use only the arms to move through the water. Pull buoys are available in a variety of shapes. Most involve two cylinder-shaped floats connected by a strap. They are made of styrofoam, foam rubber or plastic.

A buoy is worn between the thighs, with one float in front and the other behind (or above and below when horizontal in the water). The connecting strap is squeezed between the thighs. The buoy should fit snuggly so not to shift while swimming. It is important to remember not to kick while using a pull buoy.

A common difficulty with pull buoys is their tendency to slide toward the knees as the swimmer moves through the water. This can often be corrected by adjusting the connecting strap so the buoy fits more snuggly.

Pull buoys should be used sparingly in workouts. Swimmers that do not have a strong kick may find it easier to swim with a pull buoy. Some use a buoy so much that they become uncomfortable swimming without one. Over use of a pull buoy results in a weak kick and poor body position. Pull buoys should be used to allow the swimmer to focus on their arm stroke and strength. They should be used only after the swimmer has good body position, a sufficient kick and the upper body strength to accommodate the rotation of the shoulders without rotating the hips.

Most fitness pools provide pull buoys. If not, pull buoys can be purchased at most swim shops or sporting goods stores.

HAND PADDLES

Hand paddles are devices that fit over the hand and create an artificially large surface that pushes against the water during the stroke. Some are made of plastic and attach to the hands with straps or rubber bands, others look like gloves with fabric stretched between the fingers.

Hand paddles are a good way to build upper body strength. Because the paddles create a larger pushing surface, they can increase the speed of the swimmer through the water. They also increase the amount of effort needed to complete a stroke.

Paddles may also help swimmers adjust their hand motions to maximize stroke efficiency. The paddle will exaggerate any inefficient movement and make it more apparent to the swimmer.

Since they cover the palm of the hand and fingers, excessive use may cause a swimmer to lose their "feel" for the water. That is, the swimmers ability to gauge the efficiency of their stroke.

By creating an artificially large pushing surface, hand paddles can place a great deal of stress on the shoulders and elbows.

The "glove" version of the paddle creates the added complication of encouraging swimming with the fingers apart. With the gloves on, spreading the fingers creates a larger swimming surface. This can create a habit of swimming with the fingers spread when not wearing paddle gloves. The most efficient way to swim is with the fingers together. Spreading the fingers creates an inefficient stroke.

Paddles should be used sparingly to correct specific aspects of the stroke and only after the swimmer is experienced swimming without paddles.

Fitness pools occasionally supply hand paddles. If your facility does not, paddles can be purchased at most swim shops.

DRAG SUITS

Swimming suits that are designed to purposely add weight to a swimmer are called *drag suits*. These resemble the "boxer" style swimwear discussed earlier. The purpose of a drag suit is to add resistance in the water and thus make swimming more difficult. This in turn increases strength and endurance.

By creating excess resistance in the water, drag suits can place additional stress on the shoulders and elbows. Drag suits should be used only by experienced swimmers and only on a limited basis.

CAPS

Swimming caps fit snuggly over the head. They are designed to keep the hair in place and assist in streamlining the body in the water.

Caps are an effective way to keep their hair out of their eyes and away from the mouth and nose when breathing. Hair is also a source of drag in the water. By wearing a cap a swimmer can prevent their hair from needlessly slowing them down. Any swimmer with hair long enough to cover the eyes should wear a cap. Swimmers with shorter hair may choose to wear a cap to assist in streamlining.

Caps can also provide limited protection from the effects of the elements on the hair. Caps provide effective protection from the sun. However, caps do not prevent the hair from getting wet. Hair that is held under a cap will be exposed to any chemicals in the pool water.

Caps should have a smooth exterior that is free of obstructions. Caps are often printed, but three-dimensional designs and decorations should be avoided as they create drag in the water. The cap should fit snuggly over the head. Some swimmers prefer to have their ears inside the cap, other prefer to have them out. This is a matter of preference and does not impact the effectiveness of the cap. The strap of the goggles should be worn on the outside of the cap to allow easy removal.

Caps can be used as a safety device when swimming in open water. A brightly colored cap will alert boaters to the presence of a swimmer in the water.

FINS

Swimming fins are worn on the feet to increase the power of the kick. Kicking with fins uses the muscles of the legs differently than kicking without fins. Use of fins can improve flexibility of the ankles and knees. It also exaggerates flaws in the kick mechanics, offering a chance to make corrections.

Short fins should be used. Fins that are too large tend to slow the rate of the kick. The kick rate when using fins should be the same as when swimming without fins.

Fins can increase the power of the kick and help a swimmer move faster through the water. There can be a tendency to use fins too much, making swimming without them feel awkward. Fitness swimmers should use fins sparingly, if at all.

Swim fins are available at most sporting goods stores. Some facilities provide fins to fitness swimmers. These are the same types as those used when snorkeling or scuba diving, though the fins used when swimming should be smaller. If the fins are too large, they can be cut off to the proper size for the swimmer.

TOWELS

While they are not actually used in the water, towels are a necessary part of the equipment used when swimming for fitness.

Some facilities provide towels to their patrons. If not, bath-size towels should provide enough surface area to adequately dry off after swimming. A second towel can be used to dry off after showering. Using towels with a unique design will help distinguish them from the towels of other swimmers. The locker room can become very confusing when everyone uses identical towels.

SUMMARY

The only equipment needed to swim is a suit, goggles and water. Pull buoys, kick boards and other types of equipment can provide options when structuring a workout. However, they are not required for a swimming program.

If other equipment is used, make sure that it is good quality, safe and used according to the manufacturer's instructions.

Chapter Four—Structuring a Workout

TYPES OF SWIMMING WORKOUTS

Swimming features two basic types of training: *speed* training and *endurance* training. These names can be somewhat misleading because *speed* training in the water is also very beneficial to endurance.

The benefits of endurance training include a reduced blood pressure, less fatigue in daily life and increased physical strength. Endurance work elevates the heart rate for extended periods of time.

Speed training builds greater physical strength than endurance training. It can also push the heart rate higher than endurance swimming, though for shorter periods of time.

A good swimming program includes both types of training. The mix of speed and endurance will depend on the fitness goals of the swimmer.

Since the arms are the primary source of propulsion in the water, swimming puts more emphasis on upper body strength than some other forms of exercise. Swimming also tends to be less stressful on the joints because the primary source of resistance is the water rather than gravity.

When designing a fitness strategy, it is important to define how often to exercise and how long each session should be. At the beginning of a fitness program, it may be wise to swim no more than 2–3 times per week, with each session lasting long enough to effectively fatigue the body, but not push it to exhaustion. As the body adjusts to the level of activity and the unique physical challenges of a swimming workout, the amount of time spent in the pool can be increased along with the frequency and intensity of the workout sessions.

TERMINOLOGY

There are terms and practices that have developed over time that allow swimmers to communicate training concepts universally.

Swimming workout sessions are referred to as *workouts*. Workouts are made up of a series of *sets*. A set is a specific number of repetitions of a certain distance on a specified time interval. This is also known as *interval training*. Distances are displayed in terms of yards or meters (whichever applies to the pool being used) and are referred to as *reps* or *repetitions*. The time interval is described as minutes and seconds.

Below is an example of a typical set.

5 X 100 @ 2:15

This example includes 5 *repetitions* of 100-yard swims (the *distance*) on 2 minutes and 15 seconds (the *interval*). In interval training, the distance should be covered in less than the specified interval and the remaining interval is used as a rest period. In this example, the 100-yard swims begin every 2 minutes and 15 seconds. If the distance can be covered in 1:45, the swimmer will have 30 seconds to rest before starting the next repetition. The pace clock described in Chapter 2 is used to keep the swimmer on schedule.

Occasionally the repetition is given further definition. Workouts may call for specific strokes (sets can be assumed to be freestyle unless otherwise specified). The reps may also be specified as *kicking* (using only the legs), *pulling* (using only the arms) or *swimming* (using both the arms and the legs).

Breath Work is sets designed to improve the swimmer's ability to hold their breath. These are also beneficial to general conditioning.

Workouts can also include *drills*. Drills are a variation on strokes used to emphasize a particular aspect of the stroke. They can be used to improve flexibility and stroke efficiency. Examples of drills are include in the Appendix of this book.

Workouts also include *easy swims*. Easy swims are short distances that allow swimmers to recover from a difficult set (known as a *hard swim* or a *hard set*) and keep their muscles and joints flexible. Easy swims also assist in reducing stiffness after a workout.

Varied or *combination sets* can include a number of types of sets. These may include kicking, pulling, drills, breath work, etc.

Length Vs *Lap*: There has long been a controversy over the terms *length* and *lap* as they apply to swimming. A *length* in commonly defined as the distance from one end of an object to the other. A *lap* is defined as a complete circuit, covering an entire distance and returning to the starting point. Using these definitions, swimming a *length* would mean to swim from one end of the pool to the other. A lap would be to swim from one end of the pool to the other and back again, returning to the starting point.

Unfortunately, swimming is not always the most logical of environments. In swimming terms, *lap* and *length* are used interchangeably. Both terms mean to swim from one end of the pool to the other. Thus in a 25-meter pool, two laps are 50 meters and two lengths are also 50 meters.

STRUCTURING WORKOUT SETS

It is vital to have a workout planned before entering the pool. The workout can be modified while in process, but there should always be a plan before beginning. The need to modify workouts will be less frequent as swimmers grow accustomed to the process.

Workouts should be structured around the fitness goals that have been established (weight loss, appearance, general fitness, etc.). Workouts should be challenging, but the distances and intervals should be achievable.

Swimming workouts are a collection of sets. Each set has a specific goal. Some sets are endurance oriented while others are speed/strength oriented. Workouts are typically organized as follows:

Warm-up
Endurance sets
Easy swim
Varied sets
Speed sets
Cool down

The warm-up is used to get the body ready to exercise. Swimming requires substantial flexibility in the muscles and joints. The warm-up can begin before entering the pool with some basic stretching. Examples of stretching exercises are listed in the Appendix of this book.

A warm-up generally begins with some easy swimming and/or drills with steadily increasing effort. The amount of warm up an individual swimmer will need varies with the swimmer, but should rarely exceed ten minutes. The warm-up should prepare the swimmer for the workout without causing substantial fatigue.

After warming up, endurance sets should challenge the body's stamina. Endurance sets feature fewer repetitions of longer distances. The term "longer" is relative to the swimmer's ability. Suffice to say that the longest distances of the workout should be in the endurance sets.

Many fitness swimmers prefer to do only endurance work. They may design workouts that feature long periods of continuous swimming. While this type of workout can be beneficial from an endurance standpoint, it can be very fatiguing mentally. Also, after the body becomes accustomed to a particular type of workout, the benefits are limited to maintaining the level fitness that it has attained. By varying the sets that are in a workout, a swimmer can constantly challenge their level of fitness without increasing the amount of time devoted to the workout. Swimming, kicking, endurance and speed sets should be included in any workout routine (though they do not all have to be included in the same workout).

A key to endurance swimming is to establish a *pace.* That is, to swim nearly the same speed through the entire distance. The pace clock can be used to monitor speed. A worthy goal is to complete each repetition of the endurance set in nearly the same amount of time. Pace can be monitored during the swim by checking the pace clock while taking a breath. Checking the clock on the first breath after turns at the starting end of the pool is a good way to monitor pace. Some quick math will determine the amount of time taken for each two-length portion of the swim. For example, assume that a 200-yard swim starts when the clock reads ":00". (A 200-yard swim is 8 lengths of a 25-yard pool) At the end of the first two lengths the clock reads ": 50"; at the end of the fourth length the clock reads ":45"; at the end of the sixth length the clock reads ":42" and after the eighth length the clock reads ":40". In this case, the first 50 yards took 50 seconds to swim, the second 50 yards took 55 seconds, the third took 57 seconds and the fourth took 58 seconds. The total time for the entire 200-yard swim was 3 minutes and 40 seconds (Written as "3:40")

Endurance sets should be challenging. The swimmer should be substantially fatigued at the end of the set.

It is customary to follow endurance sets with an easy swim. This allows the body to recover from the set and prepare for the next set. Easy swims are generally 2 or 4 lengths of the pool.

Varied sets can be used to transition from endurance to speed sets. These include kicking, pulling, drills and other types of workout sets. A common misconception is that varied sets should not be difficult. These sets should be as challenging as any other part of the workout.

Speed sets are usually more repetitions than endurance sets and feature shorter distances. Speed sets are almost exclusively swimming. The purpose of a speed set is to swim the distance in as little time as possible (as fast as possible). The time taken for each repeat may increase as the body becomes more fatigued and the swimmer has difficulty maintaining speed, though the interval should remain constant. The speed sets should also be followed by an easy swim.

The cool down relaxes the muscles after the workout and helps prevent stiffness. The cool down is often an extended easy swim.

A specified rest interval can be inserted between sets. This is the time taken to recover from the previous set and prepare for the next set.

It can be interesting to end the workout with a particularly difficult swim. This can be a set or a single swim. The set should be very challenging. An example would be to swim 100 yards as fast a possible at the end of the workout. This trains the body and mind to rise to challenges when fatigued. These "challenge" sets are excellent motivators and fitness measurements.

As swimmers become more accustomed to writing and swimming workouts, it will become possible to literally plan every minute of a workout.

Here is an example:

	Total Distance	Total Time
Warm-up 300 @ 8:00	300	8:00
3 X 300 @ 5:00	900	15:00
1 X 100 Easy @ 3:00	100	3:00
4 X 100 Kick @ 2:30	400	10:00
8 X 50 @ 1:20	400	10:40
100 Cool down @ 4:20	100	4:20
Totals	2200	51:00

In this example, the swimmer completed a 2200-yard workout in 51 minutes. As with all workouts, the distances, repetitions, and intervals can be adjusted to the skill level of the swimmer. This type of planned workout allows the swimmer to know in advance exactly what they wish to swim and exactly how long it will take.

OTHER TYPES OF SETS

There are a number of varieties of sets that can be used to enhance a workout. Here are a few examples:

In *descending sets,* each repetition is completed slightly faster than the previous one. This is very beneficial to both strength and conditioning. It is also a very good tool for developing a sense of *pace.* Pace is an awareness of how fast you are swimming and your ability to maintain a constant speed when fatigued. The goal of a descending set is to swim each repetition *slightly* faster than the previous one. The goal is not to swim very slowly on the first few and very quickly on the last one.

Here is an example of a descending set:

5 X 100 @ 2:00 Descending

In this case each 100-yard swim is slightly faster than the previous one.

1. 1:30
2. 1:27
3. 1:23
4. 1:20
5. 1:17

Progressive swims involve gradually increasing speed through the entire distance. An example would be a 400 yard swim that is progressive by 50's. In this case, the swimmer checks their time every 50 yards. The time for each 50 should be less then the previous 50 through the entire distance.

Here is an example of a 400-yard swim, progressive by 50's:

First 50:	:50
Second 50:	:48
Third 50:	:47
Fourth 50:	:45
Fifth 50:	:43
Sixth 50:	:42
Seventh 50:	:41
Eighth 50:	:39

A *negative split* involves swimming the second half of the distance faster then the first half. The swimmer checks their time with the pace clock at the halfway point.

Swimmers can check their time with the pace clock while swimming by glancing at the clock when taking a breath or while turning at the wall.

Broken swims are divided into segments. For example, a 500-yard swim may be broken at each 100 for 10 seconds. In this case the swimmer stops at 100, 200, 300 and 400 yards and rests for 10 seconds.

Breath control is the ability to control how often a swimmer takes a breath while swimming. This can be of great benefit as it conditions the muscles to function at reduced oxygen levels.

Establishing a breathing pattern is a part of any stroke. Breath control exercises are specifically designed to enhance the body's ability to perform with limited oxygen. This is of great benefit in maintaining a breathing pattern in routine swims and also adds to the endurance aspects of the workout.

A breathing pattern may be to take a breath every other stroke (or every third or fourth), or to breath no more than twice per length (or three times, or four times, etc)

Staggered breathing is a common breath control exercise. This involves establishing a breathing pattern that changes with each length of the pool. For example, a swimmer may breath every stroke cycle on the first length, every other on the second length, every third on the third length and so on. A *stroke cycle* is all of the motions that take both arms though a complete swimming stroke.

A variation of staggered breathing is to limit the number of breaths per length. For example, the swimmer may breath 5 times on the first length, four times on the second, three times on the third, etc.

Another popular method is to swim a set of short distances (25 or 50 yards/meters) and taking as few breaths as possible, or applying the staggered breathing techniques previously described.

Breath control can be very difficult when first used. In most cases, the body readily adjusts to this form of training and improvement can be seen very quickly.

As a point of safety: Breath work should only be attempted by swimmers that have advanced to the point of comfort with the distance, speed and repetitions of swimming workouts. Excessive breath control work can cause dizziness. Beginning swimmers should use little if any breath control in their workouts.

Mixing strokes is a common way to enhance the benefits of a swimming workout. Workouts are generally made up of freestyle (crawl) swims. Swimming a variety of strokes uses the muscles in different patterns. This enhances strength, flexibility and coordination and helps to make workouts interesting.

The Individual Medley (a.k.a. IM) is a swimming race that involves all four of the recognized strokes. Equal distances are swum of the butterfly, backstroke, breaststroke and freestyle. Using all of the strokes in the same event involves changing body position and using different muscle groups. This is a great benefit to strength, endurance and flexibility.

Variations of the IM are limited only by the imagination. If a swimmer is not comfortable with the butterfly, the first quarter of the distance can be a different stroke or can be eliminated altogether. Combinations can follow any pattern.

Note that mixing strokes may be difficult in a crowded pool. Strokes other than freestyle should be used only when conditions permit.

Workouts should be planned to provide the type and level of exercise desired by the swimmer. No single workout will cover everything. Workouts should be designed to compliment each other and achieve results. If a swimmer is working out 3 times per week, the three workouts together should support the swimmer's goals. The swimmer's schedule may not allow enough time in each session for endurance, speed, kicking, pulling, drills and breath work. These can be spread across several workouts to provide a full slate of activities.

Here is an example of a week of workouts:

Day 1	Day 2	Day3
300 Warm up @ 8:00	300 Warm Up @ 8:00	300 Warm up @ 8:00
5 X 200 Descending @ 3:30	2 X 300 @ 5:00	2 X 400 @ 7:00
1 X 100 Easy @ 4:00	4 X 50 Drills @ 1:15	1 X 100 Easy @ 4:00
5 X 100 Kick @ 2:30	3 X 200 Breath Cntrl @ 5:00	5 X 100 Kick @ 2:30
10 X 25 @ :45	8 X 50 @ 1:15	3 X 100 IM @ 2:00
200 Cool Down @ 5:00	200 Cool Down @ 5:00	200 Cool Down @ 5:00
Total:	Total:	Total:
2350 @ 54:30	2200 @ 53:00	2200 @ 49:30

ESTABLISHING INTERVALS

The interval used in a set should provide enough time to complete the distance and just enough rest to prepare for the next repetition. The interval should not be long enough to completely recover from the previous swim. The interval will vary with the ability and condition of the swimmer. A good goal is 10–15 seconds rest per hundred yards/meters swum with a maximum of 45 seconds total. Intervals should be challenging, but not impossible. Swimmers should be winded from the previous repetition when starting the next.

ORGANIZING WORKOUTS FOR MULTIPLE SKILL LEVELS

Swimmers who train independently occasionally have an opportunity to join with others during a workout. This very beneficial to the training process as it allows and exchange of ideas and training philosophies as well as adding to the enjoyment of the workout session.

To gain the benefits of shared workouts; swimmers must begin and end each set together. If possible, the workout should be designed to allow the swimmers to start and end each repetition together. This is accomplished by using sets with the same intervals and adjusting the distance for each swimmer's speed.

Below are examples of coordinated workouts for three swimmers of different speeds. Note that the intervals are nearly identical and the distances have been adjusted for each swimmer.

Swimmer 1	Swimmer 2	Swimmer 3
300 Warm up @ 8:00	200 Warm Up @ 8:00	200 Warm up @ 8:00
5 X 200 Descending @ 3:00	5 X 150 Descending @ 3:00	5 X 100 Descending @ 3:00
1 X 100 Easy @ 4:00	1 X 100 Easy @ 4:00	1 X 100 Easy @ 4:00
3 X 150 Kick @ 2:30	3 X 100 Kick @ 2:30	1 X 200 Kick @ 7:30
10 X 50 @ 1:00	6 X 50 @ 1:30	6 X 50 @ 1:30
200 Cool Down @ 5:00	200 Cool Down @ 5:00	200 Cool Down @ 5:00
Total:	Total:	Total:
2300 @ 49:30	1850 @ 49:30	1250 @ 49:30

It is important to remember that in fitness swimming the relative speed of the swimmers is less important than the effort put into the workout and the fitness benefit derived from the workout. Speed through the water is a method to measure the results of the workout, but is not the absolute measurement of fitness. Each swimmer should train at the level appropriate for them.

MEASURING PROGRESS

As with any initiative, progress is measured against the goals that have been established (weight loss, appearance, fitness, swimming ability, etc.) Some type of measurement must be established to monitor progress.

As discussed earlier, it is vital to be aware of the goals of the fitness program. The goals determine what type of program should be developed. The most important measurement is against the overall goals of the program.

Measurement must be convenient and meaningful. If the goals involve more difficult measurements such as blood pressure or cholesterol levels, it may be appropriate to identify interim goals that are more convenient to measure.

Below are some examples of goals and how to evaluate progress.

Weight:

If one of the goals is to lose or control body weight, a good practice is to record the weight on a regular basis. Weight should be checked at the same time each day. The most accurate body weight is taken in the morning, before breakfast. The weight recorded in the morning reflects the weight of the body, with normal fluid levels and an empty stomach.

Do not record body weight immediately after a workout. The act of working out artificially reduces the weight of the body. Often the body weight is affected by the difficulty of the workout. This will distort the results.

It is important to note that there is a period of time at the beginning of a fitness program when you may not lose weight or even gain weight due to increased muscle mass. This is a good thing, it will inevitably cause the body to burn more calories and weight loss will be more dramatic.

Heart Rate:

One of the best indicators of general fitness is heart rate. An easy measurement is to count the pulse at the throat or the wrist for 6 seconds and multiply by 10. The result is an approximate 1-minute heart rate.

The first benchmark is the *resting pulse*. The resting pulse is the rate the heart beats under the minimum of stress. A common method to estimate the resting pulse is to take a 6-second count of the heart rate first thing in the morning. A true resting pulse should be taken while sleeping, but this can be rather difficult to obtain. A close approximation is to take the pulse immediately after waking.

The resting pulse can be used in two important fitness measurements. The first is general fitness. The resting pulse will decrease as the heart becomes stronger and more efficient. Periodically monitoring the resting pulse gives an indication of the direction of general fitness.

The resting pulse can also be used to determine the amount of effort for a set or workout. By taking the pulse during a workout and comparing it to the resting pulse, a swimmer can determine the relative effort of a set. The pulse after a set is known as the *working pulse*.

Another effective measurement is the recovery after a hard set. The *recovery pulse* is the heart rate following a set and a specified amount of rest, usually one minute. The *recovery* is the difference between the *working pulse* and the *recovery pulse*. The greater the difference between the working pulse and the recovery pulse, the higher the level of fitness.

To review:

The *resting pulse* is the heart rate at rest.

The *working pulse* is the heart rate after exercise (in swimming terms, this is after a set.) The greater the difference between the resting pulse and the working pulse, the greater amount of effort.

The *recovery pulse* is the pulse one minute after the exercise has stopped. The greater the difference between the working pulse and the recovery pulse, the higher the level of fitness.

Swimming Ability

Tracking the progress of swimming ability can be a good indicator for other goals. As the general level of fitness improves, swimming work-out will require less effort. As speed and efficiency improve, intervals will provide more rest and should be adjusted to keep the workouts challenging.

Swimming speed is usually defined as the amount of time taken to swim a specific distance. As strength, endurance and stroke mechanics improve the speed through the water increases.

A more formal measurement of speed is a scheduled *swim for time*. This is a pre-determined distance that is swum periodically and the performance times compared. A swimmer may schedule a timed swim for the last Friday of each month. The workout that day will include a single swim or set that is particularly challenging. The time for the swim is noted and compared to previous performances.

The *swim for time* should be the same distance or set on each occasion for a valid comparison. If the distance or set is changed (as is often the case a swimming ability improves), it can only be compared to other swims of the same distance.

A swimmer may schedule a 200-yard swim for time on the last day of each month. The time for the swim is compared to previous months. The results can be logged in a table that might look like this:

Date	Time
1/31	3:12
2/28	2:58
3/31	2:49
4/30	2:45
5/31	2:43
6/30	2:40

Note that the time improves more quickly in the early months. This is not uncommon. It is possible to achieve great gains in the first few weeks of a program. Performances tend to level off as fitness improves.

Distance:

As the body becomes more fit and accustomed to swimming workouts, it will become possible to swim more distance in the same amount of time. A good measurement of this is to track the total distance of a workout session. Below is an of a swimmer's record for 1-hour workouts example:

Date	Distance
1/31	2300
2/28	2500
3/31	2800
4/30	3000
5/31	3100
6/30	3200

This is a somewhat less refined measurement, but is still a good indicator of progress.

STAYING MOTIVATED

Motivation is key to any fitness program. It can also be the most challenging. Below are some suggestions to help stay focussed on the goals.

Success

A little success goes a long way. There are few motivators with more impact than success. Experiencing progress toward goals is an invaluable motivator. Measurement of progress is key. Establish a routine for measuring progress and use the results.

Lack of success can also be a motivator. It may inspire greater effort or changes in the program.

Set "Interim" goals

Goals can be established at any time. A swimmer can decide at any time to set a goal for a repeat, a set, a workout or a series of workouts.

Challenge Yourself

Place a particularly difficult or fast swim at the end of the workout, just before the cool down. This will provide a target to work toward during the workout. It also trains the body to perform when fatigued.

Keep a logbook

Some swimmers record the detail of the entire workout, including the sets and the performances. Some merely keep track of total distance. Whatever the case, a logbook will help keep a program on track. Keeping a detailed record of workouts will also create a library of ideas that can be referred to for future workouts.

Another use of a logbook is to track total distance over a period of time. Some swimmers monitor weekly totals while others may track year-to-date distance. A good motivational tool is to convert the distance into miles with a goal of an imaginary trip, like swimming to Hawaii. (Or, if you happen to live in Hawaii, swimming to another place) Find the distance to the desired location and keep a running total of the distance in each workout. Convert the distance to miles and track progress toward the destination. (One mile is approximately 1760 yards)

Adjust the approach

A benefit of a program designed for an individual is that it is very easy to implement changes. Change can originate in many different circumstances. It may be triggered by achieving the initial goals or it may be the result of less satisfactory results.

Adjusting the workout routine through experience and experimentation can keep a fitness program fresh and help to keep interest in the program at a high level.

Use your imagination

Some swimmers find it helpful to imagine that they are in a close race and their competition is in the lane next to them. Some even identify their competition as someone they don't like. This is particularly helpful on difficult or challenging sets.

Try Competition

Preparing for competition is an excellent way to stay motivated. Competitive events are available for swimmers of all skill levels. There are a number of venues where adult swimmers and test their skills in competition. United States Master Swimming is a popular organization that sponsors competitive event s throughout the USA. There are similar organizations in other countries. Contact the staff at a swimming facility for information on a local Masters organization. Information on Masters programs is also available on the Internet.

Chapter Five—Stroke Mechanics

S troke mechanics are the physical movements of a swimmer's body that propel them through the water. A swimmer training alone may have some difficulty evaluating their stroke mechanics because they are not able to view themselves as they swim. There are several techniques that can assist swimmers in evaluating and improving their strokes.

It is important to note that no text can substitute for face to face instruction. This text is intended to help swimmers that are comfortable swimming and may need assistance with the finer points of the strokes. Those with serious stroke deficiencies should seek assistance in the form of swimming instruction.

BASIC CONCEPTS

The traditional view the motions of swimming is placing the hands in the water in front of their body and moving them through the water to the end of the stroke and then placing them back to the point where they started. Actually, the hand enters the water and remains in the same place, the motions of the hand and arms move the body over the hand, thus propelling the body forward.

Compare this concept to running. The runner places their foot in front of their body. The foot remains in the same place as the muscles of the leg move the body over the foot and propel it forward. The same concept applies to swimming, the main difference being that the swimmer's hand slips through the water rather than staying in the same place as a runner's foot does. The goal of stroke mechanics is to minimize how much the hand slips through the water. This improves the stroke's efficiency, thus moving the body forward faster and with less wasted motion.

A swimming stroke is divided into two sections: the *pull* and the *recovery*. The *pull* is the motion that provides the propulsion and the *recovery* returns the hands to the starting position (relative to the body). The pull is further divided into three sections: the *catch*, the *dig*, and the *push*.

The *catch* is the point at which the hand enters the water. The hand and lower arm act as a paddle that grabs a point in the water and attempts to stay there. The *dig* begins the forward motion and brings the shoulders over the hand. The *push* completes the propulsive portion of the stroke by bringing the torso and hips over the hand. The *recovery* brings the hand to point in front of the body where it can catch new water. The completion of this process with one arm is known as a *stroke*. The completion of this process with both arms is called a *cycle* or *stroke cycle*. When swimming freestyle (a.k.a. *Crawl*), a single stroke cycle includes two strokes, one with each arm.

The kick serves two functions. By keeping the feet at the surface of the water, the kick helps to maintain body position. The kick can also provide substantial forward motion.

One key to an efficient stroke is to find "still water". As the hand pushes against the water, the water immediately in front of the hand begins to move with the hand. If the hand continues to move in a straight line, the water in front of the hand continues to move and the stroke looses traction in the water. This is the same affect as swimming upstream or running on a treadmill. In swimming this is known as *slipping*.

By moving the hand slightly up, down, left or right, the hand will find water that is not moving ("Still Water"). After catching that water, the hand must move again to find more still water. The process continues through the entire pull. Swimmers often refer to the ability to find still water as a "feel for the water". The process of moving the hand to find still water is called *sculling*.

Sculling is used in all of the strokes. The hand moves up, down and to the side as part of the stroke pattern. Sculling is used extensively by synchronized swimmers. Synchronized swimmers move their hands back and forth in the water to maintain position and to move in any direction.

A good exercise for sculling is to *tread water*. Treading water is to hover in water that is deep enough that the swimmer cannot stand on the bottom. Standing upright in the water with arms extended to the sides, a swimmer can maintain their position by quickly moving the hands back and forth about 8–10 inches, just below the surface of the water. The palm of the hand is turned in the direction that the hand is moving and angled slightly downward. This may take some practice, but is a good way to develop the sculling motion.

Another key aspect of efficient strokes is the direction of the propulsive force. Force should always be directed backward. Any motion that pushes water a direction other than backward is counter-productive.

The hands and forearms act as "paddles" when swimming. A swimmer's goal is to create the largest possible paddle to push against the water. The hand should be relaxed with the fingers together.

BODY POSITION AND STREAMLINING

An essential factor in efficient swimming is the position of the body in the water. The term *streamlining* refers to minimizing the resistance to forward motion. For maximum efficiency, the leading edge of a swimmer's body should be as small as possible. This allows the swimmers body to "push" as little water as possible. The greater the surface area pushing on the water, the greater the resistance of the water.

Proper body position is horizontal in the water, with the head and shoulders as the leading edge. The hips, legs and feet should flow behind the head and shoulders as close to the surface of the water as possible.

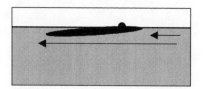

Proper Body Position
The leading edge of the body is small, minimizing the amount of water that must be pushed out of the swimmers way.

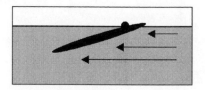

Poor Body Position
The leading edge of the body is large, increasing the amount of water that must be pushed out of the swimmer's way.

Strokes

This text addresses the finer points of stroke mechanics for the free-style, backstroke and the dolphin kick.

The Freestyle (also known as the "Crawl" stroke) should be used for the majority of fitness swimming. It is the easiest stroke to learn the stroke that provides the greatest control over direction and the greatest ability to see around the pool.

The backstroke can provide a viable alternative to the freestyle for easy swims and combination sets.

The dolphin kick (the kick used with the butterfly stroke) is an excellent exercise for the stomach, hips and back.

FREESTYLE

Body Position

The body is face down in the water; the back is slightly arched. The head is tilted at a 45-degree angle with the eyes focused on the bottom of the pool, ahead of the swimmer. The head should break the water at about the hairline. The stroke should feel as if there is a cable attached to the forehead that is pulling the body through the water.

Arm Stroke

The hand enters the water in front of the body, slightly to the outside of center, with the arm at full extension. The shoulder rolls down and forward, tuning the upper body on its side. This extends the hand further in front of the body. The head does not rotate. After catching the water, the hand moves down into the water and away from center. The arm is turned so the elbow points up and out. As the hand passes the shoulder (which ends the dig phase), it turns back toward the body and passes under the hips. The hand is then pushed along the thigh until the arm is fully extended. The shoulder rolls back to push the hand further down the body, ending the push phase.

The hand and forearm together form a paddle that can push against the water and propel the swimmer forward. The paddle starts at the elbow and ends at the fingertips. To employ the entire paddle while swimming it is important to keep the elbow high during the "dig" phase. The hand should lead the arm through the stroke. This is relatively easy to monitor because the swimmer can view the "dig" portion of the stroke.

Keeping the elbow high in the dig phase also allows the body to engage additional muscle groups in the stroke. A low elbow (a stroke that leads with the elbow) depends upon the muscles of the back and underarm to provide the force behind the stroke. A high elbow (a stroke that leads with the hand) brings the muscles of the chest into the dig portion of the stroke, greatly increasing the propulsive force.

The recovery brings the hand out of the water with the elbow high and pointing up. The shoulder rolls up (coinciding with the shoulder roll of the other arm as it "digs"). The hand passes close to the body and re-enters the water at nearly full arm extension. The shoulder rolls down and forward to begin another stroke.

The alternating arm strokes should work in rhythm with each other. Each arm should move smoothly through the stroke without stopping.

Kick

The feet move up and down opposite each other. The propulsive force is on the downward portion of the kick. This is known as a *flutter* kick.

The kick originates at the hip. The knees and feet move up and down opposite each other while the hips remain horizontal (No rotation of the hips). A good way to visualize the kick is to imagine that a piece of tape is stuck to your toe and you are trying to kick it off. The knees are slightly bent on the downward motion and nearly straight on the upward motion. The toes are pointed and the feet point slightly inward (slightly pigeon-toed). The feet should move up and down about 8 to 12 inches and lightly break the surface of the water.

There are two basic rhythms for freestyle kick. The two-beat kick involves kicking each foot once per stroke (thus, two beats per cycle). The six-beat kick is six kicks per cycle. The two-beat kick essentially keeps the feet at the surface of the water, which assists in maintaining the proper body position without using very much energy. The six-beat kick helps to maintain body position as well as provide forward motion.

Breathing

Turn the head to the side during the push portion of the stroke. Take a breath of air and return the head to its proper position during the recovery portion of the stroke. Slowly exhale through the nose and mouth while the face is in the water.

Do not lift the head to breathe. Lifting the head forces the feet downward. As the feet sink, they create drag on the body and stop all forward motion. The head should turn to the side without being lifted further out of the water.

Breathing to both the left and the right (known as *bi-lateral breathing*) is crucial to a balanced and smooth stroke. Breathing exclusively to one side can lead to excessive shoulder roll that disrupts body position and alters the stroke rhythm.

A good method to develop bi-lateral breathing is to take a breath on every third arm pull. For example, turn the head to the right during the push of the right arm. Exhale through strokes of the left arm and the right arm, then turn the head to the left as the left arm pushes. It may feel awkward at first, but with practice it becomes very smooth and the benefits to the stroke efficiency are immeasurable.

No matter how smooth the breathing motion, it still impacts the body position. Competitive swimmers put great effort into limiting their breathing.

Turns

The act of turning around at the end of the pool is referred to as *turns*. One basic freestyle turn is known as the *open turn*. In the open turn, the swimmer touches the wall with the hand and uses the hand as a point of leverage to spin the body around, bringing the feet to the wall. After taking a breath, the swimmer pushes off of the wall with the arms over the head and resumes swimming.

A faster method of turning is known as the *flip turn* or *tumble turn*. This turn involves tucking the body into a ball just before reaching the wall, spinning forward (head down) to bring the feet over to the wall. Then pushing off of the wall with the arms over the head and turning face down to resume swimming.

The mechanics of a flip turn can be broken into defined steps.

1. Approach the wall with both hands at the sides. This is accomplished by not doing the recovery portion of the final strokes.

2. At the appropriate distance from the wall, kick downward with both feet while tucking the head down and bend at the

hips. With the palms turned downward, bend the arms at the elbow to bring the hands from the sides in front of the body to a position near the shoulders.

3. The motions of step 2 should bring the feet up and over as the body performs a summersault. Bend at the knees as the feet come out of the water.

4. As the feet reach the wall, extend the hands over the head. At this point, straighten the body and push off of the wall. Focus on the opposite end of the pool and turn the body face down to resume swimming.

Note: the "appropriate distance from the wall" varies with the height and speed of a swimmer. Through experimentation the proper distance can be found.

Glide

Swimmers can take advantage of the force provided by pushing off the wall by momentarily gliding through the water. The glide is accomplished by stretching the body toward the opposite end of the pool. Hands together, over the head, face down, feet together, toes pointed. The body should be about 6–8 inches below the surface of the water.

The swimmer should begin kicking shortly after pushing off of the wall (as the force of the push diminishes and the swimmer slows in the water). Use the first pull to bring the body back into the proper position. With practice a swimmer can transition from glide to kick to swim without losing momentum.

The position of the head controls the body's depth while gliding. If the head is tilted toward the surface, the body will rise. If the head is tipped down, the body will move deeper into the water.

As a rule, swimmers should never, ever, *ever*, take a breath on the last pull before a turn or the first pull after a turn. Taking a breath immediately before the turn alters the body position and interferes with monitoring the distance from the wall as the head turns to breathe.

The first pull after the turn should return the body to a proper swimming position. Turning the head to breathe lifts the head too far out of the water. This forces the feet down causing drag in the water, thus losing the momentum created by the push off the wall.

Kicking in a Workout

A kick board is usually used. (Details on kick boards can be found in Chapter 2) The board should be held in front of the swimmer. The arms should be extended over the board with the hands grasping the board at the front. The back should be arched with the hips just below the surface of the water. The head should be held slightly more upright than when swimming. Eyes focused ahead. The water should break over the nose just below the eyes. The swimmer should lift the head to take a breath and then return to the proper position. Do not push down on the kick board to maintain body position. The kick board should be used for stability while the kick provides forward propulsion.

For a more challenging set, try kicking without a kick board. This is both physically challenging and a test of mechanics. When kicking without a kick board, the upper body should remain stable in the water and not rotate with each kick.

COMMON PROBLEMS IN FREESTYLE

Poor Body Position

This is usually a combination of carrying the head too high and the feet too low. This creates excessive drag that forces a swimmer to swim harder to cover the same distance. Make sure that the head is held so that the water breaks across the forehead. The kick should be strong enough to keep the feet no more than 8 to 12 inches below the surface of the water.

Short Strokes

Short strokes are the result of not extending the arms fully at the beginning and/or at the end of the stroke. A great deal of the power of a stroke comes from the catch and the push. A short stroke does not take advantage of this power. Drills such as one-arm swims and catch-up strokes can help correct this problem. Descriptions of these drills are in the Appendix of this book.

Another aid in correcting short strokes is to count the number of strokes taken in each length of the pool. As the stroke becomes longer and more efficient, the number of strokes per length will be reduced.

Exaggerated Breathing

Some swimmers alter their strokes when taking a breath. These swimmers often lift the head when taking a breath or keep the face out of the water for an extended period. This results in a hesitation or pause in the stroke. Turning the head to breathe should not alter the rhythm of the stroke. The head should be turned just far enough to take a breath.

Some swimmers hold their breath while swimming and try to exhale *and* inhale when the head is turned. Exhaling underwater during the stroke clears the lungs so that the swimmer only needs to inhale while the head is turned.

With practice, the breathing process can be streamlined to minimize the impact on the form and rhythm of the stroke.

Too Much Kick

Some swimmers lift their feet completely out of the water when kicking. Lifting the feet completely out of the water uses energy and alters the body position without providing any propulsive force. The feet must remain in the water to move the body forward. Lifting the feet out of the water creates a lot of splash behind the swimmer, giving he appearance of a powerful kick. However, it actually reduces the amount of forward power.

Bending the knees while kicking often causes this exaggerated kick. The knees should be bent only slightly during the down stroke of the kick and nearly straight during the up stroke.

Low Elbows

The dig portion of the stroke requires that the elbows be turned up and away from the body. This allows the hand to lead the stroke and the hand and forearm to push against the water and engages the muscles of the chest and forearm in the motion. The elbows pointing downward indicate that the elbow is leading the stroke. This reduces the power of the stroke and allows the hand to slip through the water without catching.

Swimmers can observe the catch and dig portions of the freestyle. When swimming, watch the hand and arm to make sure that the elbow is high.

Straight Arm Recovery

The recovery portion of the stroke returns the hand to the starting place in front of the body. The proper recovery involves bending the elbow to keep the hand near the body. This streamlines the stroke and maintains the forward momentum. A straight-arm recovery creates side-to-side motion that impacts the stroke by altering the body position and creating motion in a direction other than forward.

Insufficient Shoulder Roll

When swimming freestyle the shoulders should roll from side to side with each stroke. This allows the arm to extend further at the beginning and the end of the stroke and brings the arm into the proper position for the recovery. It also brings the muscles of the shoulder and back into the motion. Insufficient shoulder roll limits the motion and the muscle groups involved in the stroke.

BACKSTROKE

Body Position

The body is face up in the water; the back is slightly arched. The head is held as if standing with good posture. The eyes should focus directly above. The top of the head should break the water. The stroke should feel as if there is a cable attached to the top of the head that is pulling the body through the water.

Arm Stroke

The hand enters the water in above the head (in front of the swimmer as they move through the water), slightly to the outside of center, as close to full arm extension as possible. The little finger enters the water first and the palm is turned away from center. The shoulder rolls down, turning the upper body on its side, extending the hand further forward. The head does not rotate. After catching the water, the hand moves down into the water and away from center. The arm is turned so the elbow points down. As the hand passes the shoulder (which ends the dig phase), it turns back toward the body and passes under the hips. The hand is then pushed down and along the thigh until the arm is fully extended. As the arm reaches full extension, the hand is turned palm-in, with thump up.

The recovery brings the hand out of the water, thumb first with palm turned toward the body. The elbow is straight. The shoulder rolls up (coinciding with the shoulder roll of the other arm as it "digs"). The hand passes over the body with the elbow straight. As the arm passes vertical, the hand is turned palm-out. The hand re-enters the water at nearly full arm extension, little finger first and the palm out to begin another stroke.

The alternating arm strokes should work in rhythm with each other. Each arm should move smoothly through the stroke without stopping.

When swimming backstroke, it is impossible to see the bottom of the pool or the pool in front of the swimmer. To swim in a straight line, find a landmark in the pool area to use as a guide. This can be a line on the ceiling, a light fixture, a sign, anything that can be used as a reference point.

Most pools have flags across the pool 5 yards or meters (whichever applies to that particular pool) from the end of the pool to help backstrokers locate the wall when they are swimming. The lane lines usually change color at this point as well. By counting the number of strokes from the flags to the wall, a backstroker can approximate the location of the wall even though they cannot see it.

Turning the head to the side or straight back will help to locate the wall, though this has a serious impact on body position and the efficiency of the stroke.

Kick

The backstroke kick is very similar to the freestyle kick. The feet move up and down opposite each other. The propulsive force in backstroke is on the upward portion of the kick.

The kick originates at the hip. The knees and feet move up and down opposite each other while the hips remain horizontal (No rotation of the hips). A good way to visualize the kick is to imagine that a piece of tape is stuck to your toe and you are trying to kick it off. The knees are slightly bent on the upward motion and nearly straight on the downward motion.

Kicking in a Workout

Kicking for backstroke does not require a kick board. Lying face up in the water, place the hands directly over the head, just below the surface of the water, palms up. Place one hand on top of the other and grasp the hands together. Use a landmark in the pool area to kick in a straight line as with swimming. The flags across the pool 5 yards/ meters from the wall can help approximate the location of the wall, though it may be somewhat more difficult as there are no strokes to count. When all else fails, turn the head and look!

Breathing

Breathing patterns on backstroke are unique in that the face is never fully submerged, though there is considerable wash and spray across the face. An established breathing pattern will help maintain the rhythm of the stroke and allow the swimmer to concentrate on other aspects of the stroke. The most common breathing pattern for backstroke is to inhale while one arm is pulling and exhale when the other arm is pulling.

Turns

There are three types of backstroke turns.

- The Open Turn
- The Barrel Turn
- The Flip Turn

The open turn is similar to that of the freestyle. The swimmer touches the wall with the hand and uses the hand as a point of leverage to spin the body around, bringing the feet to the wall. After taking a breath, the swimmer pushes off of the wall and resumes swimming.

The barrel turn takes this a step further. As the hand grabs the wall, the swimmer raises the head slightly. The knees are bent and brought toward the chest, lifting the feet out of the water. Using the hand as a leverage point, the swimmer quickly spins the body so the feet come to rest on the wall. The swimmer then places the arms over the head, tilts the head back and pushes off the wall to resume swimming.

The flip turn is the fastest of the turns. The swimmer uses the last stroke before reaching the wall to turn over, face down in the water. The swimmer then executes a flip turn as described for freestyle with one minor change. Instead of turning face down after the turn, a backstroker remains face up after the turn, pushes off the wall and resumes swimming backstroke.

Glide

Swimmers can take advantage of the force provided by pushing off the wall by momentarily gliding through the water. The glide is accomplished by stretching the body toward the opposite end of the pool, face up, hands together, over the head, feet together, toes pointed. The body should be about 6–8 inches below the surface of the water. Gently exhaling through the nose will keep water out of the nose during the glide.

The position of the head controls the body's depth while gliding. If the head is tilted toward the surface, the body will rise. If the head is tipped down, the body will move deeper into the water.

The swimmer should begin kicking shortly after pushing off of the wall (as the force of the push diminishes and the swimmer slows in the water) and use the first pull to bring the body back into the proper position. With practice, swimmers can transition from gliding to kicking to swimming without losing speed.

Backstrokers may choose to use a dolphin kick while gliding under the surface. (An explanation of the dolphin kick appears later in this chapter)

COMMON PROBLEMS WITH BACKSTROKE

Poor Body Position

The proper body position in backstroke includes arching the back. Many swimmers attempt to swim backstroke bent at the waist (In a sitting position). This creates a great deal of drag and literally pulls the body down. The back should be arched with the hips just below the surface of the water.

Leading with the Elbow

The dig portion of the stroke requires that the elbows be turned down and away from the body. This allows the hand to lead the stroke, the hand and forearm to push against the water and engages the muscles of the chest and forearm in the motion. If the elbow is pointing toward the feet, the elbow is leading the stroke. This reduces the power of the stroke and allows the hand to slip through the water without catching.

Exaggerated Kick

Some swimmers lift their feet completely out of the water when kicking. The feet must remain in the water to provide propulsive force. Moving the feet through the air does not provide any forward movement. While this type of kicking creates a lot of splash behind the swimmer, it actually reduces the amount of forward power.

Bending the knees while kicking often causes this exaggerated kick. The knees should be only slightly bent during the up stroke of the kick and nearly straight during the down stroke.

Bent Arm Recovery

The arms should be straight during the recovery. Bending the arm at the elbow causes water to wash over the face, making breathing difficult. A bent-arm recovery also makes it nearly impossible to place the arm in the water properly to begin a new stroke. A bent-arm recovery leads to a poor placement of the hand at the catch point in the stroke and causes the elbow to lead the stroke rather than the hand.

Short Strokes

Short strokes are the result of not extending the arms fully at the beginning and/or at the end of the stroke. A great deal of the power of a stroke comes from the catch and the push. A short stroke does not take advantage of this power. Drills such as one-arm swims and catch-up strokes can help correct short strokes. Descriptions of these drills are in the Appendix of this book.

Another aid in correcting short strokes is to count the number of strokes taken in each length of the pool. As the stroke becomes longer and more efficient, the number of strokes per length will be reduced.

Side-to-Side Motion

This is caused by placing the hand too far across the body to start the stroke. This is often the result of a bent-arm recovery. The hand should enter the water little finger first, just outside of center (In line with the ear). Placing the hand across the centerline causes the initial force of the stroke to the side rather than to the back. Pushing to the side causes the body to move in the opposite direction. When the other arm begins its stroke, it pushes the body to the other side. This is a very inefficient way to swim as a great deal of effort is devoted to moving side-to-side, rather than forward.

Proper placement of the hand at the beginning of the stroke allows the force of the stroke to be pushed backward, moving the body forward.

Up-and-Down Motion

Pushing downward in the initial catch of the stroke pushes the body upward. The hand can support the body in this position until is passes under the hips. At that point the body settles back to its original position. When the next stroke starts, the body is pushed up again, repeating the process. This is a very inefficient way to swim as a great deal of effort is used to push the body up.

The force of the stroke should be directed down and back, maintaining body position and pushing the body forward. If the body is moving up and down with each stroke, adjust the motion at the beginning of the stroke to direct the force backward.

Head Movement

The head should remain motionless in relation to the body. Any movement of the head will alter body position and stroke mechanics. Focussing on a landmark in the pool will help keep the head motionless as well as helping the swimmer swim in a straight line.

Insufficient Shoulder Roll

When swimming backstroke the shoulders should roll from side to side with each stroke. This allows the arm to extend further at the beginning and the end of the stroke and brings the arm into the proper position for the recovery. It also brings the muscles of the shoulder and back into the motion. Insufficient shoulder roll limits the motion and the muscle groups involved in the stroke.

DOLPHIN KICK

The dolphin kick is an excellent way to exercise the muscles of the stomach, hips, thighs and back.

The kick board should be held in front of the swimmer in the same manner used for kicking freestyle. The arms should be extended over the board with the hands grasping the board at the front. The back should be arched with the hips just below the surface of the water. The head should be held slightly more upright than when swimming. Eyes focused ahead. The water breaks over the nose just below the eyes. The swimmer should lift the head to take a breath and then return to the proper position.

In the dolphin kick the feet move up and down together. The propulsive force is created as the feet move down through the water. The kick originates just below the shoulders. As the hips move up and down, they cause a rippling effect down the legs. The hips and feet move opposite each other. As the feet move downward, the hips move up. As the feet move up, the hips move down. This may seem awkward at first, but with practice becomes very steady and rhythmic.

Dolphin kick can also be performed with the body facing up. This can be used as a kicking drill or during the glide portion of the backstroke. When performing dolphin kick on the back, the propulsive force is on the upward stroke. The kick board should not be used when kicking on the back.

TIPS FOR IMPROVING STROKE MECHANICS

The goal of improving strokes is to make them more efficient. By reducing or eliminating wasted motion and misdirected energy, swimmers are assured of using their muscles properly and avoiding undue stress on their muscles and joints.

It should be noted again that the best way to improve stroke mechanics is instruction. This text will assist in improving general stroke technique. But, it is not intended to replace learning from a qualified instructor.

The best way to improve your stroke is to observe it. Unfortunately, swimmers do not have the luxury of being able to see themselves swim.

However, there are ways for a swimmer that trains alone to evaluate and improve stroke efficiency. The key to self-evaluation is knowing what to look for and how to measure it.

There are four keys to stroke efficiency:

- Finding still water
- Long strokes
- Directing the propulsive force
- Minimizing wasted motion

Finding Still Water

Swimming strokes involve a sculling motion in the water. This provides the maximum amount of traction in the water and ensures that the swimmer is receiving the maximum forward motion from each stroke.

Long Strokes

Extend the stroke fully at the beginning and the end of the pull. This ensures the greatest possible benefit from each stroke. All strokes except backstroke allow the swimmer a limited ability to observe the forward extension. There are drills that provide the ability to measure the extension at the end of the stroke.

Directing the propulsive force

All of the propulsive force of the stroke should be directed backward, thus pushing the swimmer forward. Any force that is exerted to the side is not only wasted, but is counter-productive as it pushes the swimmer to the side, rather then forward. This factor can also be measured and addressed through drills.

Wasted motion

Any motion that does not contribute to the forward movement of the swimmer should be minimized or eliminated. These motions use energy and do not produce any benefit to the stroke.

Wasted motion includes excessive movement of the hips (which also affects body position), excessive motion to breath, awkward recovery and others.

Stroke Counts

A good test of stroke efficiency is to count the number of strokes used to swim one length of the pool. As the efficiency of the stroke improves, the number of strokes will decline.

You Learn What You Do and You Don't Learn What You Don't Do

(A.k.a.: Habit is Everything)

A crucial element improving stroke mechanics is to be aware of the stroke at all times. Every part of a workout can be considered time spent working on stroke mechanics. Good mechanics are a matter of habit. While portions of the workout may be designed to focus on mechanics, aspects of mechanics must be in every part of the workout.

Chapter Six—Pool Etiquette

C rowded pools can be very challenging places to swim. Individuals that are not aware of a few simple guidelines can compound the challenges. Swimmers have developed informal protocols that allow all participants to get the most from their time in the pool.

Etiquette does not only apply to crowded pools. Etiquette applies to any situation where the pool is shared by two or more swimmers. The purpose of etiquette is to allow all of the swimmers in the water to be able to complete their workouts with as little interruption and distraction as possible.

The first point of pool etiquette is to know the rules of the pool and follow them. The pool rules are usually posted in the pool area. Following the rules also allows the lifeguards to spend more time protecting the swimmers and less time enforcing rules.

CHOOSING A LANE

Select a lane prior to entering the water. The lane should have swimmers with abilities comparable to your own. This will allow for an even flow of swimmers through the lane.

It is important to note that the pool is available to swimmers of all abilities. Don't be overly concerned about sharing a lane with a faster or slower swimmer. If everyone follows the guidelines, swimmers of varying speeds can swim together with little difficulty.

Entering the Water

Enter the water in a way that minimizes the impact on other swimmers. The facility may prohibit diving into the pool for safety reasons. The best way to enter the water is feet first at the edge of the pool. Entry into the water should be timed so that it does not interfere with the swimmers already in the lane.

SHARING A LANE

The most convenient way to swim is in a lane alone. A single swimmer in a wide lane can concentrate completely on the workout without concern for other swimmers. Most pools have more than one swimmer per lane. Fortunately, there are methods that allow multiple swimmers to share a lane with little interference.

If the lane is wide enough, two swimmers share with one swimming on each side. The centerline can act as a divider. In this case each swimmer can complete their sets and need only be concerned with the other swimmer at the points where they meet.

Side by Side Swimming

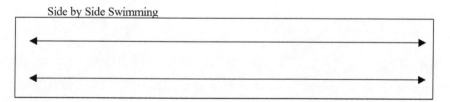

When entering a lane that already has one swimmer, it is appropriate to ask them to share the lane and which side of the lane they would prefer. Swimmers understand that sharing lanes is necessary and are usually not offended if asked. Asking to share is a polite way to let them know that they need to accommodate another swimmer. It is appropriate to wait until a swimmer stops to ask them about sharing a lane. Never interrupt a swimmer while they are swimming. If the swimmer in the lane you want to use is on a long set, it may be appropriate to enter the water when the other swimmer is not near the end of the pool. This will allow them to see the new swimmer and know that they are now sharing a lane. Assume that a side-by-side pattern is correct and begin swimming when you are sure they have seen you.

The other swimmer may not be aware of your plans. Use caution for the first few laps to ensure that both swimmers are aware of each other and what pattern is being used.

The "side-by-side" method of sharing becomes obsolete when a third swimmer enters the lane. With three or more swimmers a process known as "circle swimming" comes into play. In circle swimming, (a.k.a.: "swimming circles"), the swimmers swim on one side of the lane when swimming one direction and on the other side of the lane when swimming the other direction. Swimmers usually keep to the right. Using this method, swimmers can swim behind one another on an endless loop within the lane. Circle swimming allows as many swimmers to participate as can fill the circle.

A common error is to swim too close to the center of the lane. This causes other swimmers to move out of the way. This is not only annoying, but dangerous as it can lead to collisions.

The switch from one side of the lane to the other takes place at the end of the pool, just before executing a turn. The swimmer crosses over to the opposite side of the lane before executing the turn. This allows the swimmer to execute a turn and push off the wall without facing oncoming swimmers.

Proper Circle Swimming

Note that the swimmers move to the opposite side of the lane prior to executing the turn

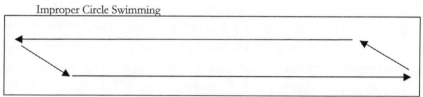

Improper Circle Swimming

Note that the swimmers execute a turn prior to moving to the opposite side of the lane.
These swimmers are pushing off of the wall while facing oncoming swimmers.

Time your entry into a lane of circle swimmers to create the least possible disruption of the other swimmers. Do not jump into the water directly in front of another swimmer.

PASSING

In circle swimming it occasionally becomes necessary for one swimmer to pass another. This can be accomplished with minimal interruption of both swimmers' workouts.

The faster swimmer carries the primary responsibility in passing. When approaching a slower swimmer, the faster swimmer can see the other swimmer as well as oncoming swimmers in the same lane. Swimmers being passed cannot see behind them.

The faster swimmer should pass to the left of the slower (In circles where swimmers keep to the right). The slower swimmer is next to the lane marker and the faster swimmer is in the center of the lane. The faster swimmer should lightly tap the foot of the slower swimmer to let them know they are about to be passed. The slower swimmer should move as close to the lane marker as possible to allow the faster swimmer more room to swim around them. After tapping he slower swimmer's foot, the faster swimmer should move slightly to the left and sprint past the slower swimmer. The faster swimmer should not move back into their normal position until they are certain that they have passed the slower swimmer.

If the lanes of the pool are wide enough, the swimmers needn't be overly concerned with oncoming swimmers. This will only be a point of concern if swimmers moving in opposite directions are being passed at the same time at the same point in the pool.

Passing in the middle of the pool

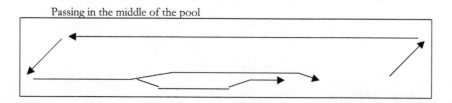

When passing during a turn, the faster swimmer should lightly tap the foot of the slower swimmer before passing. The slower swimmer limits the movement to the left prior to the turn, allowing the faster swimmer to move to their left. The faster swimmer executes a turn as close to the far lane marker as possible. After pushing off of the wall, the slower swimmer stays slightly to the left of their normal course until the faster swimmer has completed the pass.

Passing at the turn

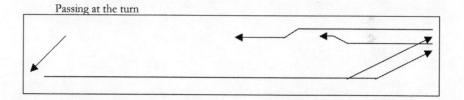

RESTING IN THE POOL

When not swimming, it is important to stay out of the way of those who are. This can be accomplished by standing near the lane line opposite oncoming swimmers. Do not stand in the center of the lane. Oncoming swimmers attempting to execute turns will not appreciate an obstacle in the center of the lane.

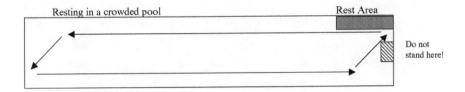

Resting in a crowded pool

Rest Area

Do not
stand here!

COLLISIONS

Swimmers in a crowded pool bump into each other. Their arms
become entangled and they disrupt each other's strokes. This is to be
expected and does not warrant excessive guilt or apologies. Most swimmers understand that collisions are a part of the workout and are not
antagonized by the event, AS LONG AS EVERYONE INVOLVED
IS USING SOUND SWIMMING PRACTICES.

The usual reaction is to keep swimming. If both parties are relatively
unhurt, both can complete their sets and exchange apologies later.

CONVERSATIONS

As discussed in earlier chapters, nearly every aspect of swimming workouts is timed. Rest periods are usually short and time for conversation
is limited. Swimmers are generally a sociable group and are willing to
carry on conversations during workouts, but the workout takes prece-
dence over almost everything else.

A swimming workout is governed by the clock. When the clock
indicates that the set should start, the swimmers start swimming
regardless of what other swimmers are doing. Consequently, swimmers
have a tendency to begin a set or a repetition in the middle of a sen-
tence. Do not be offended if a conversation is cut short because someone started swimming. The conversation will pick up again during the
next rest period. The best place for a non-disjointed conversation is
before or after a workout.

STROKE SELECTION

Any stroke is suitable if sharing a lane with one or two people. Freestyle is the only appropriate stroke in a crowded pool. It affords the most directional and speed control and allows the swimmer to best view of their surroundings.

TURNS

After executing a turn, look ahead to see if any swimmers are to your immediate front before pushing off. Swimmers that push off of the wall without looking cause many collisions.

EQUIPMENT

Many facilities provide basic equipment such as kick boards and pull buoys. These are stored in a specific place or area on the deck. Always get your own equipment from the storage area and return it when you have finished your workout. This is a matter of courtesy. Equipment that is near the pool is most likely being used by swimmers that are in the water, though they may not be using it at the moment. Equipment on the deck may also be privately owned. Returning the equipment after a workout helps to keep the pool deck orderly and safe.

DECK ETIQUETTE

The first rule of standing on the deck is not to ever block the swimmers' view of the pace clock. The pace clock governs almost all activity in the pool. Blocking the view of the swimmers disrupts their workout and is very frustrating.

In most pools, the best place to stand or stretch is along the sides of the pool, rather than at the ends. The sides of the pool provide the most room and have the least impact on those in the water. Also, the deck at the end of the pool may be wet from swimmers entering and exiting the pool. The side of the pool is more likely to have a dry area for stretching. If the end of the pool is the only space available, be sure to stand back from the edge of the pool.

When stretching, make sure that you have sufficient room to complete the exercises without interfering with anyone on the deck.

IN THE LOCKER ROOM

If the facility has a variety of locker sizes, select the proper size for your needs. Don't use an extra large locker if you only have a few items. This will leave the larger lockers available to those who need them.

Keep the dressing area dry. Most locker rooms have an area near the showers that can be used to dry off. Use this area to prevent tracking water into the dressing or locker area. Keeping the floor dry will make the locker room more clean and comfortable. Clothes that fall on the floor will not get wet. This also has safety benefits as the floor will be less slippery.

Chapter Seven—Common Ailments

S wimming, like most physical activities, can produce minor conditions specific to the exercise. While the vast majority of fitness
swimmers will never experience any of these conditions, it is important
to understand them and be prepared if they do appear. This chapter
identifies common ailments and makes suggestions to avoid and treat
them.

Many of these ailments can be attributed to the environment in
which swimmers train. Emersion in water affects the hair, skin and
eyes. Swimming outdoors adds other elements such as sun and wind to
the environment.

Other common ailments are similar to those associated with other
forms of exercise. These include minor pain in the muscles and joints.

It should be noted that these ailments tend to be minor in nature
and are more annoying than debilitating. These are no more serious
than the ailments associated with other forms of exercise. A physician
should address more serious ailments such as excessive joint or muscle
pain.

THE DIFFERENCE BETWEEN "GOOD PAIN" AND "BAD PAIN"

"Good" pain is associated with working the muscles and pushing them
beyond previous limits. This is the mild stiffness and soreness that follows physical activity. This type of pain is a dull ache that is limited to

the muscles used in the exercise. It subsides as the body becomes accustomed to the activity. Good pain is mild and does not interfere with normal daily activity.

Good pain for swimmers can be located in any part of the body, but is usually limited to the muscles of the upper arm, chest, upper back, shoulder or thigh.

Good pain, though a sign of success in the workout, is still uncomfortable. Stretching prior to the workout and an effective cool down and a hot shower or whirlpool after the workout are excellent ways to avoid or limit good pain.

One of the best treatments for good pain is activity. Re-working the stiff muscles aids in reducing discomfort. Also, good pain subsides as the body becomes accustomed to the exercise. The more often the muscles are used, the faster they become accustomed to the level of activity. If the pain is severe enough to interfere with your daily routine, it may be advisable to limit your next workout or include additional drills and easy swims.

"Bad" pain is the result of an injury or over exertion. This is a sharp pain in the muscles or joints. It may also take the form of muscle pain that is severe enough to interfere with daily activity.

Bad pain can be a sign of progressing too quickly into a strenuous fitness routine. Fitness routines must start with mild exercise and gradually become more challenging. Bad pain can be avoided by reducing the level of exertion in the workout and gradually building it back up.

Changing the workout structure, the frequency of the workout or the mechanics of the stroke are other treatments for bad pain.

The workout structure can be changed to include a longer warm-up, shorter distances, additional kicking sets or fewer "hard" sets. The frequency of the workout could also be a factor. More frequent workouts of short distances may be better than fewer workouts of greater distance.

Stroke mechanics may also play a part in the cause of bad pain. Poor stroke form may place undue stress on the joints. Correcting the stroke pattern may relieve this stress and thus remove the pain.

In rare cases pain may be a sign of injury. Consult a physician if severe pain persists for more than a few days.

STOMACH PAIN

Mild abdominal pain is generally part of the conditioning process. These are commonly referred to as stomach cramps. These cramps rarely persist for more than a few workouts.

The best way to avoid a cramp is to begin a program with mild exercise and gradually increase the intensity. Stomach cramps may be a sign that the program is progressing too quickly. Reduce the intensity of the workout until your body has adjusted.

Stomach pain may also be the result of swimming too soon after a meal. Any physical exertion immediately after eating can result in stomach pain. The best way to prevent this type of cramping is to avoid swimming less than one hour after a meal.

MUSCLE CRAMPS

A muscle cramp is a sudden, uncontrolled tightening of a muscle. Muscle cramps usually strike swimmers in the calf or in the arch of the foot. These types of cramps are generally limited to the early weeks of a program. Muscle cramps are less likely as the body becomes accustomed to the level of activity.

A reliable treatment for a muscle cramp is to relax and stretch the affected muscle. Move to an area where the water is shallow enough to stand or, ideally, get out of the water. If the cramp has struck the calf or foot, bend the knee of the affected leg, grab the ball of the foot with both hands and gently straighten the leg while pulling on the ball of the foot. The cramp should relax as the leg straightens. Gentle massage after the muscle has relaxed can also help. If the cramp returns, repeat the process. It is not unusual for a cramp to return several times before it subsides. A warm shower, hot tub or whirlpool bath can also help to relieve a leg cramp. Any discomfort should subside shortly after the muscle relaxes.

A cramp in the lower leg should signal the end of your workout. Competitive swimmers often continue swimming after a muscle cramp. However, fitness swimmers, particularly those that are early in their program, should end their workout when a muscle cramp strikes.

THE EFFECTS OF THE ELEMENTS

Water in the ear

Swimming can cause water deposits to accumulate in the ear canals. This is not only uncomfortable; it can also lead to painful ear infections. Water should be removed from the ear as soon as possible after swimming.

There are a number of ways to remove water from the ears. The simplest is to tip the head quickly to the side. If this does not work, a few drops of rubbing alcohol in the ear will help remove the water. There are also a number of non-prescription medications for water in the ear.

There is another very effective, though rather unorthodox, method to remove water from the ear canal.

To remove water from the left ear, stand upright in a dry floor with good footing. Steady yourself with a hand on a wall or other suitable object. Raise the right foot. Tilt the head slightly to the left. While jumping up and down on the left foot, move the head to the left with a jerk. Repeat the process for the right ear if necessary, jumping on the right foot. (I have no idea why this works, but I have never known it to fail).

Dry Skin

Swimming, like any other activity in the water, washes the natural moisturizers from the skin. Without these substances, the skin can become dry, itch and flaky. Excessive bathing or showering can have the same effect.

In addition to the effects of the water, many of the chemicals used in pools act as drying agents on the skin. Showering after swimming will remove these chemicals from the skin.

The natural moisturizers washed away by the water must be replaced. Most moisturizing lotions do an excellent job. Apply the lotion liberally over the entire body as soon after showering as possible.

Maintaining proper hydration by drinking plenty of fluids can assist the body in naturally replacing lost moisture.

Damaged Hair

The effects of water on the hair are similar to the effects it has on the skin. Pool chemicals such as chlorine have a more profound effect on hair. With prolonged exposure, chlorine can act as a bleaching agent on the hair. This is similar to the effects of prolonged exposure to the sun. The hair can lighten in color and may become brittle. These effects are usually minor and are directly proportional to the amount of time spent in the pool. (A person that swims 10 hours per week will see more effects than someone that swims 5 hours per week.)

A swimming cap will reduce the effects, but will not eliminate them. The best prevention is to wash the hair immediately after swimming with a quality shampoo and rinse thoroughly. There are a number of shampoos specially formulated for swimmers.

Eye Irritation

Exposing the eyes to water can wash out the eye's natural lubricants. To counter this, the eyes increase the amount of lubricants, thus creating a "watery" look in the eyes. Pool chemicals can cause irritation to the sensitive tissues in the eye.

The best way to prevent eye irritation is to wear goggles. Goggles can prevent 100% of the irritation associated with exposure to pool water. Goggles should fit snuggly and comfortably around the eye.

Eye irritation can be treated with eye drops that provide moisture and reduce irritation. Avoid drops that only reduce "redness". Many of these reduce redness by restricting the flow of blood through the eye. Restricting the blood flow can increase eye irritation rather than relieving it.

A cool washcloth placed on the eyes can also reduce discomfort.

Effects of the sun

Swimming in bright sunlight has the same effect on the skin and hair as any other activity in the sun. The water in the pool does not protect the skin and hair from the effects of the sun. Waterproof sunscreen can help protect the skin. Wearing a swimming cap can protect the hair from sun damage. Showering and shampooing after swimming will also reduce the effects of the sun and water.

Bright sunlight can also contribute to eye irritation. Tinted goggles have shaded lenses similar to sunglasses and can lessen the effect of the sun.

Colds

A nagging ailment that afflicts many athletes is a recurring common cold. While there is no cure for common colds, there are ways to avoid them.

- Wear a hat on cold days. Being outdoors or in a vehicle on cold days with wet hair is an invitation to a cold.

- Wear a coat on cold days. Being outdoors or in a vehicle on cold days without a coat is an invitation to a cold.

- Keep the immune system strong. The body can fight off a number of illnesses if given the proper tools. A proper diet and plenty of sleep will help maintain a strong immune system.

- Drink plenty of fluids. Maintaining proper levels of liquids will help cleanse the body tissues.

Experimentation with these and other preventative measures and treatments can help determine what works for you.

Appendix I Stretching

Comments on stretching:

Stretching is designed to limber the muscles and joints to prepare them for exercise. Stretching should be a smooth motion, extending to the point of full extension and then slowly releasing. Do not "bounce" or force the motion beyond full extension. Muscles and joints should feel better after stretching than they did before stretching.

Basic stretches:

1. Arm Swings I: Begin with the arms extended to the front at shoulder height. Swing the arms backward until the hands meet behind your back, keeping the hands at shoulder level. (Your hands may not meet the first few time you do this, keep trying)

2. Arm Swings II: Begin with your arms at your sides, feet slightly apart. Swing the arms one at a time in a windmill motion, both clockwise and counter clockwise. Do this slowly at first and steadily faster.

3. Arm Swings III: Begin with your arms at your sides, feet slightly apart. Swing the arms in a windmill motion in the same direction opposite each other (as if swimming). As the arms swing, roll the shoulders to the front and back without turning the hips. Swing the arms forward to simulate freestyle and backward to simulate backstroke.

4. Arm Swings IV: Stand with feet slightly apart. Bend slightly at the waist. Move the arms through simulated freestyle strokes, rolling the shoulders with each stroke.

5. Coordination Arm Swing: Begin with your arms extended over your head. Swing both arms as described in Arm Swings II, moving one arm clockwise and the other counter clockwise at the same time. Reverse the arms after a few rotations. As the arms swing, roll the shoulders to the front and back without turning the hips.

6. Arm Stretches I: Place the right arm behind the head with the right hand touching the left shoulder. The right elbow should be pointing straight up. Grab the right elbow with the left hand and pull it to the left. This should stretch the muscles under the right shoulder. Repeat the process for the left arm.

7. Arm Stretches II: Place the right arm in the starting position described in Arm Stretches I. Grab the right wrist with the left hand and push it to the right. This will stretch the muscles on the back of the right arm. Repeat the process for the left arm.

8. Floor Stretch: Sit on the floor with legs straight in front. Place the right foot on the outside of the left knee. Twist at the waist so the right hand can be placed on the floor on the outside of the right foot. Place the left hand on the floor behind you. Continue to twist to full extension, turning the head to the left. Release and repeat to the other side.

9. Leg /Back Stretch I: From a standing position, spread the feet as far apart as is comfortable. Bend at the waist, reaching for the floor. After touching the floor, reach between the legs to touch the floor as far behind you as possible.

10. Leg/Back Stretch II: Stand with the feet together. Bending at the waist, reach down as far as possible toward the toes. Do not bounce, keep a steady stretch as far as possible and release slowly.

11. Leg Stretch: From a standing position, step forward with the right foot, bending at the right knee. Place the hands on the floor on each side of the right foot (for balance). Place the left foot, with left knee straight, as far behind you as possible. Repeat with the left foot in front.

Appendix II Drills

Overview

Drills can play a very important part in any swimming program. Swimming drills serve a number of purposes.

- They often include only a portion of the full stroke, which allows the swimmer to concentrate on that portion of the stroke.

- They often exaggerate the motions of a stroke, which enhances joint and muscle flexibility.

- They improve the efficiency of the stroke by ensuring that the propulsive force is directed correctly

- They often alter the body position, allowing the swimmer to observe portions of the stroke that cannot usually been seen when swimming.

The following pages describe some common stroke drills. These can be incorporated into a warm up, used as a separate set or used in the cool down. This list contains only a portion of the drills that have been developed. Swimmers often create their own drills to fit a specific need in their program.

Name of Drill: **Water Polo Stroke**

Description: Swim freestyle with the head held completely out of the water, facing forward with the water breaking under the chin

Notes: Lifting the head out of the water will force the feet down, creating a slightly upright position in the water. Strong swimmers may be able to execute this drill without kicking.

Benefits:

- Strengthen the upper body

- Improved stroke efficiency

- Allows the swimming to view the hand entering the water, the catch, the dig and a portion of the recovery

Points of Emphasis:

- The head should be held steady, facing forward

- The hand enters the water at nearly full extension and slightly outside of center

- Roll the shoulders as when swimming

- Fully extend the arm in front at the beginning of the stroke

- Catch the water and move the hand through a normal freestyle stroke

- Keep the elbows high

- Fully extend the stroke at the end of the push

Common Mistakes:

- Do not shorten the stroke at either end of the pull

- Do not move the head with each stroke. The head should be held steady, looking forward.

Name of Drill:	**One Arm Freestyle**
Description:	Swim facedown with the hands held in front of the head at full extension (at the point of the catch). Using only one arm, complete the entire stroke cycle, holding the other arm in front. Use the same arm for an entire length of the pool and the other arm on the next length
Notes:	Breath no more than every other stroke

Benefits:

- Stroke efficiency-Swimming with one arm exaggerates the effect of misdirected motion. Some swimmers will find it difficult to swim in a straight line with one arm. This is a sign that propulsive force is being sent a direction other than backward.
- The ability to isolate and concentrate on the mechanics of each arm individually

Points of Emphasis:

- A strong kick will maintain body position through the drill
- The hand enters the water at nearly full extension and slightly outside of center
- Fully extend the arm in front at the beginning of the stroke
- Catch the water and move the hand through a normal freestyle stroke
- Keep the elbows high
- Fully extend the stroke at the end of the push
- Roll the shoulders to bring the arm out of the water for the recovery
- Breath to the right when using the right arm, to the left when using the left arm
- Concentrate on swimming in a straight line

Common Mistakes:

- Swimming in a circle indicates that the initial catch and dig are pushing to the side rather than to the back. Swimmers should move in a straight line while swimming with one arm.

Name of Drill: **Catch-Up Freestyle**

Description: Swim face down with the hands held in front of the head at full
                        extension (at the point of the catch). Using only one arm, complete
                        the entire stroke cycle, keeping the other arm in front. When one
                        arm has completed an entire stroke cycle, repeat the process with
                        the other arm. Arm strokes alternate for the entire distance of the
                        drill.

Notes: Breath no more than every other stroke

Benefits:

- Stroke efficiency

- The ability to isolate and concentrate on the mechanics of each
  arm individually

Points of Emphasis:

- A strong kick will maintain body position through the drill

- The hand enters the water at nearly full extension and slightly
  outside of center

- Fully extend the arm in front at the beginning of the stroke

- Catch the water and move the hand through a normal freestyle
  stroke

- Keep the elbows high

- Fully extend the stroke at the end of the push

- Roll the shoulders as when swimming

- Breath to the right when using the right arm, to the left when
  using the left arm

- Concentrate on swimming in a straight line

Common Mistakes:

- Swimming from side to side indicates that the initial catch and
  dig are pushing to the side rather than to the back.

Name of Drill:	**Head-Down Freestyle**
Description:	Swim freestyle with the head down, looking backward under the body.
Notes:	Breath as little as possible. Exhale through the nose

Benefits:

- Stroke efficiency

- Coordination with kick

- The ability to see the push portion of the stroke, the kick and the body's position in the water.

Points of Emphasis:

- The hands should reach full extension at the end of the stroke

- The kick should be neither too large nor too small

- Maintain proper body position

Common Mistakes:

- Rotating the hips

- Moving the shoulders from side to side rather than rolling the shoulders on the center axis

Name of Drill:	**One Arm Backstroke**
Description:	Swim face up with the hands held in over the head at full extension (at the point of the catch). Using only one arm, complete the entire stroke cycle, holding the other arm over the head in the starting position. Use the same arm for an entire length of the pool and the other arm on the next length
Notes:	Maintain a strong kick through the entire drill

Benefits:

- Stroke efficiency

- The ability to isolate and concentrate on the mechanics of each arm individually

Points of Emphasis:

- A strong kick will maintain body position through the drill

- The hand enters the water at nearly full extension and slightly outside of center

- Fully extend the arm in front at the beginning of the stroke

- Catch the water and move the hand through a normal backstroke

- Keep the elbows high

- Fully extend the stroke at the end of the push

- Roll the shoulders to bring the arm out of the water for the recovery

- Keep the elbow straight on the recovery

- Place the hand in the water at the starting point with the palm out.

Common Mistakes:

- Swimming in a circle indicates that the initial catch and dig are pushing to the side rather than to the back. Swimmers should move in a straight line while swimming with one arm.

Name of Drill:	**Catch-Up Backstroke**
Description:	Swim face up with the hands held in over the head at full extension (at the point of the catch). Using only one arm, complete the entire stroke cycle, keeping the other arm in front. When one arm has completed an entire stroke cycle, repeat the process with the other arm. Arm strokes alternate for the entire distance of the drill.
Notes:	Maintain a strong kick through the entire drill

Benefits:

- Stroke efficiency

- The ability to isolate and concentrate on the mechanics of each arm individually

Points of Emphasis:

- A strong kick will maintain body position through the drill

- The hand enters the water at nearly full extension and slightly outside of center

- Fully extend the arm in front at the beginning of the stroke

- Catch the water and move the hand through a normal backstroke

- Keep the elbows high

- Fully extend the stroke at the end of the push

- Roll the shoulders to bring the arm out of the water for the recovery

- Place the hand in the water at the starting point with the palm out.

Common Mistakes:

- Swimming from side to side indicates that the initial catch and dig are pushing to the side rather than to the back.

Name of Drill:	**Dead-off Swims**
Description:	Swim a specified number of lengths of the pool, purposely turning before reaching the end of the lane.
Notes:	Turning before reaching the end of the pool denies the swimmer the benefit of pushing off of the wall. This forces the swimmer to begin swimming from a dead stop, with no forward momentum.

Benefits:

- Increased stroke efficiency

- Increased physical strength (Upper body and legs)

- Increased power in the first stroke after a turn

Points of Emphasis:

- Turn as close to the wall as possible without touching it

- Use a few powerful strokes with a strong kick to begin forward motion

Common Mistakes:

- Taking too many strokes to get up to normal speed

- Not kicking

Name of Drill:	**Sculling**
Description:	Position the body vertically in water that is deep enough that the swimmer cannot touch the bottom of the pool. Extend the arms out to the sides, palms down. Use a flutter kick (the kick used for freestyle). Move the arms back and forth in the water, turning the palm slightly in the direction of the motion. The hands should move about 12 inches and remain just below the surface of the water.

Notes:

This drill should keep the head out of the water without using any downward strokes

Benefits:

- Arm strength

- Improved stroke efficiency (use of sculling motion when swimming)

- Improved "feel" for the water

Points of Emphasis:

- Keep the elbows pointed up and back

- The hands should remain at the surface of the water

- The head and neck should be out of the water

- The hands should move no more than 12 inches forward and backward

Common Mistakes:

- Using a kick other than the flutter kick

- Using downward strokes to stay afloat

Variations:

Perform the drill without kicking. Keep the legs straight with toes pointed toward the bottom of the pool

Name of Drill:	**Vertical Kicking**
Description:	Position the body vertically in water that is deep enough that the swimmer cannot touch the bottom of the pool. Arms may be extended to the side for balance or kept to the sides, hands on thighs. Using a flutter kick (the kick used for freestyle), keep the head out of the water without using the arms.
	This drill can be used as a single, timed exercise (i.e. for 30 seconds) or as a set (30 seconds of kicking, 30 seconds of rest, repeated)
Notes:	This drill should keep the head out of the water without any arm strokes

Benefits:

- Leg strength

- Improved kicking form

Points of Emphasis:

- The head should stay in a constant position, not move up, down, backward or forward

- The back should be slightly arched to keep the body perpendicular in the water

- The head and neck should be out of the water

- The feet should not move more than 12 inches forward and backward

Common Mistakes:

- Bending at the waist

- Using the arms

- Using too broad a kick

Name of Drill:	**Underwater Dolphin Kick**
Description:	Push off the wall, face up, as if beginning the backstroke. Keeping the body 8–12 inches below the surface, use dolphin kick to move through the water as far as possible. The arms should be over the head with hands together.
	Use a backstroke arm stroke to raise the body to the surface for a breath.
	After surfacing, use backstroke or a drill to reach the end of the pool.

Notes:

- Slowly exhaling through the nose will keep water out of the nose.
- Exaggerate the movement of the hips for added benefit.
- The position of the head controls the body's depth in the water. If the head is tilted toward the surface, the body will rise. If the head is tipped down, the body will move deeper into the water.

Benefits:

- Leg strength
- Strong stomach
- Improved kicking form
- Breath control

Points of Emphasis:

- The head should remain at a constant depth (not move up and down)
- The back should be slightly arched
- The head and neck should be aligned with the body (the head should not be tipped up or down)
- The feet should not break the surface of the water

Common Mistakes:

- Bending at the waist
- Kicking too far below the surface of the water
- Kicking too close to the surface of the water

Appendix III Sample Workouts

The workouts described on the following pages are designed for swimmers of all fitness levels. Intervals have been omitted from the workouts to allow swimmers to assign intervals that they are comfortable with.

These workouts are meant as guides and suggestions to help swimmers design workouts that are interesting and challenging. They can be used as presented or modified to suit each swimmer's goals.

Workouts are made up of sets. Each of the sets described here can be combined with sets from other workouts to create a new approach.

1000 YARDS/METERS

Warm up 200 Build-up
4 X 100 Swim
1 X 100 Kick
4 X 50 Swim
100 Cool Down

Warm up 100 Swim
       4 X 50 Drills
1 X 200
1 X 100
2 X 50 Kick
4 X 50
100 Cool Down

Warm up 100 Swim
        2 X 50 Drills
3 X 150 Swim
3 X 50 Kick
3 X 50 Swim
1 X 100 Kick
100 Cool Down

Warm Up 100 Swim
        2 X 50 Drills
1 X 200 Swim
2 X 100 Pull
1 X 100 Kick
1 X 50 Easy
3 X 50 Swim
100 Cool Down

Warm up 200 Build-up
1 X 300 Swim
1 X 200 Kick
1 X 100 Pull
2 X 50 Swim
100 Cool Down

Warm up 4 X 50 Drills
2 X 200 Swim
3 X 100 Kick
100 Cool Down

2000 YARDS/METERS

Warm up 200 Build-up
5 X 100 Swim
2 x 50 Drills

5 X 100 Swim (Faster than 1st 5 X 100)
2 X 50 Drills
4 X 100 Kick
200 Cool Down

Warm up 100 Swim
          100 Pull
          100 Kick
1 X 500 Swim
1 X 400 Swim
1 X 300 Swim
1 X 200 Swim
1 X 100 Swim (Average time per 100 must drop with each)
200 Cool Down

Warm up 200 Swim
2 X 50 Drills
4 X 150 Swim
1 X 100 Kick
4 X 100 Swim
1 X 100 Pull
6 X 50 Swim
1 X 100 Kick
100 Cool Down

Warm Up 100 Swim
          4 X 50 Drills
2 X 300 Swim
1 X 50 Easy

3 X 200 Swim
1 X 50 Easy
3 X 100 Swim
100 Cool Down

Warm up 500 Build-up
4 X 200 Swim
2 X 200 Kick
4 X 50 Swim
100 Cool Down

Warm up 100 Swim
         4 X 50 Drills
5 X 100 IM
4 X 100 Kick (one each stroke)
5 X 100 Swim
1 X 50 Easy
3 X 50 Very Hard
100 Cool Down

3000 YARDS/METERS

Warm up 300 Build-up
5 X 100 Swim
4 x 50 Drills

5 X 100 Swim (Faster than 1st 5 X 100)
4 X 50 Drills
5 X 100 Kick

5 X 100 Swim (Faster than 2nd 5 X 100)
300 Cool Down

Warm up 200 Swim
           200 Pull
           200 Kick
1 X 500 Swim
1 X 400 Swim
1 X 300 Swim
1 X 200 Swim
1 X 100 Swim (Average time per 100 must drop with each)
4 X 100 Kick
4 X 50 Hard
300 Cool Down

Warm up 200 Swim
4 X 50 Drills
4 X 200 Swim
1 X 100 Kick
4 X 150 Swim
1 X 100 Kick
4 X 100 Swim
1 X 100 Kick
6 X 50 Swim

1 X 100 Kick
100 Cool Down

Warm Up 200 Swim
        200 Pull
2 X 500 Swim
1 X 50 Easy
3 X 200 Swim
1 X 50 Easy
4 X 100 Swim
1 X 50 Easy
4 X 50
250 Cool Down

Warm up 500 Build-up
5 X 200 Swim
2 X 200 Kick
5 X 100 Swim-Descending
2 X 100 Kick
6 X 50 Swim
100 Cool Down

Warm up 200 Swim
        4 X 50 Drills
4 X 100 Kick (one each stroke)
3 X 200 IM
4 X 100 Kick
4 X 100 IM
5 X 100 Swim-Descending
1 X 100 Easy
2 X 50 Very Hard
100 Cool Down

4000 YARDS/METERS

Warm up 400 Build-up
5 X 100 Pull or Swim
4 x 50 Drills
5 X 100 Swim (Faster than 1st 5 X 100)
4 X 50 Drills
5 X 100 Kick
5 X 100 Swim (Faster than 2nd 5 X 100)
1 X 100 Easy
5 X 100 Kick
6 X 50 Descending
300 Cool Down

Warm up 200 Swim
       200 Pull
       200 Kick
1 X 100 Swim
1 X 200 Swim
1 X 300 Swim
1 X 400 Swim
1 X 500 Swim
1 X 400 Swim
1 X 300 Swim
1 X 200 Swim
1 X 100 Swim
3 X 200 Kick
300 Cool Down

Warm up 200 Swim
4 X 50 Drills
5 X 200 Swim
3 X 100 Kick

4 X 150 Swim
3 X 100 Kick
5 X 100 Swim
3X 100 Kick
6 X 50 Swim
3X 100 Kick
100 Cool Down

Warm Up 200 Swim
            200 Pull
3 X 500 Swim
2 X 50 Easy
3 X 200 Swim
2 X 50 Easy
5 X 100 Swim
2 X 50 Easy
10 X 50 Swim
200 Cool Down

Warm up 300 Build-up
3 X 300 Swim
3 X 100 Kick
4 X 200 Swim
3 X 100 Kick
4 X 100 Swim
4 X 100 Kick
8 X 50 Swim
200 Cool Down

Warm up 200 Swim
            4 X 50 Drills
            200 Pull
4 X 100 Kick (one each stroke)
4 X 200 IM

4 X 100 Kick
5 X 100 IM
1 X 100 Easy
4 X 100 IM
1 X 100 Easy
4 X 50 (one each stroke)
1 X 100 Easy
4 X 50 Swim (Freestyle)
200 Cool Down

5000 YARDS/METERS

Warm up 200 Swim
        200 Pull
        200 Kick
1 X 100 Swim
1 X 200 Swim
1 X 300 Swim
1 X 400 Swim
1 X 500 Swim
1 X 500 Swim
1 X 400 Swim
1 X 300 Swim
1 X 200 Swim
1 X 100 Swim
3 X 200 Kick
10 X 50 Swim
300 Cool Down

Warm up 200 Swim
        4 X 50 Drills
        200 Pull
4 X 100 Kick (one each stroke)
5 X 200 IM
4 X 100 Kick
5 X 100 IM
3 X 100 Kick
1 X 100 Easy
5 X 100 IM (Faster than 1st 5 X 100 IM)
4 X 100 Kick
5 X 100 IM (Faster that 2nd 5 X 100 IM)
300 Cool Down

Warm up 200 Swim
4 X 50 Drills
5 X 300 Swim
4 X 100 Kick
4 X 200 Swim
4 X 100 Kick
5 X 100 Swim
4 X 100 Kick
8 X 50 Swim
200 Cool Down

Warm Up 200 Swim
          200 Pull
3 X 500 Swim
2 X 50 Easy
3 X 300 Kick
5 X 200 Swim
2 X 50 Easy
3 X 100 Kick
5 X 100 Swim
200 Cool Down

Warm up 300 Build-up
6 X 300 Swim
3 X 100 Kick
5 X 200 Swim
3 X 200 Kick
4 X 100 Swim
10 X 50 Swim
100 Cool Down

Warm up 400 Build-up
1 X 1000 Swim
4 x 50 Drills

6 X 200 Swim
5 X 100 Kick
10 X 100 Swim
1 X 100 Easy
8 X 50 Descending
200 Cool Down

THE AUTHOR'S FAVORITE WORKOUT

7000 Yards/Meters

Warm Up   1000 Swim
3 X 500 Swim Descending
5 X 200 Kick   Descending
5 X 200 Swim Descending
5 X 200 Kick   Descending
5 X 100 Swim Descending
5 X 100 Kick   Descending
6 X 50 Swim   Descending
200 Cool Down

0-595-25300-8

Made in the USA
Lexington, KY
15 March 2010